THIS BOOK
BELONGS TO THE

FAMILY

Written by Mary Manz Simon
Illustrated by Fátima Anaya
Designed by Lauren Williamson

VN0003466;9781506448558;JUN2019

Beaming Books
510 Marquette Avenue
Minneapolis, MN 55402
Beamingbooks.com

THE FAMILY TIME BIBLE

by Dr. Mary Manz Simon

illustrated by Fátima Anaya

beaming books

MINNEAPOLIS

For our five grandsons:
Elijah, Solomon, Luke, Nate, and Josh

"Children's children are a crown to the aged, and parents are the pride of their children."
Proverbs 17:6 (NIV)

"My sheep know my voice, and I know them. They follow me."
John 10:27 (NIV)

TABLE OF CONTENTS

Old Testament

New Testament

HOW TO USE THIS BOOK

Family time is precious, so finding even a few minutes can be a challenge. Because eating is a social event, many families naturally gather at mealtime. Perhaps you come together during the bedtime routine. Other families celebrate "found moments," those brief times between activities or during rare "downtime." Whenever you find each other, savor the moments. Time with loved ones is a gift from God.

This easy-to-use devotional was written and designed for your busy family. If you have two minutes, five minutes, or twenty, you'll find meaningful talking points and relatable content. When time permits, you can use all the elements that accompany each story. When time is short, you might choose a single fill-in-the-blank prayer, discussion question, or fast fact. Choose what works for you, when it works for you. Some suggestions:

- Maximize the moments. Remove distractions (including screens!).

- Be flexible. There is no "magic length" for a good conversation with your child or with God.

- Relax. Discussion starters and talking points don't have a right or wrong answer.

- Be creative. Fill in and date the blanks you complete and comments you add so this volume becomes a ready-made legacy of your family's journey through the Bible.

- Enjoy! When you and your child come together with God, you are pulling together what matters most in life.

The book features fifty-two Bible stories, each with its own section. The introduction invites readers to think about the upcoming story.

When you don't have much time, a Fast Fact or two might just be enough to satisfy you!

A Bible reference sits at the top.

The story is told in an easy-to-understand style. Beautiful illustrations draw in the reader and bring the story to life.

The section called Talk about It offers discussion questions to encourage conversation around the table.

Pray Together includes a prayer with blanks you can fill in to make it your own.

The Note to Parents focuses on the theme of the story and relates it to everyday situations, providing helpful suggestions and guidance.

God bless you as you share The Family Time Bible!

MEALTIME PRAYERS

Mealtime prayers are often brief. After all, hungry children don't like to wait! And yet, even a short or simple prayer can be meaningful. Your child might like to repeat one of these prayers or use their own words.

A mealtime pause to pray can help us all remember that everything, including our food, is a gift from God. Instilling a sense of thankfulness will gradually help a child understand that gratitude flows naturally from the heart.

For food to eat
and food to share
I thank you, God,
for love and care.

Now I'll fold my hands and say,
"Thank you, God, for food today."

Let's all hold hands together
as we come here to say,
"We thank you for the blessing
of healthy food today."

My hands I fold.
My head I bow.
God bless this food,
I ask you now.
Thank you, God, I want to say
as I eat this food today.

Before I start eating,
I just want to say,
Thanks, God, for this food you
have giv'n today.

The food I see before me
was made with care and love.
I'm grateful for these blessings
you've sent from up above.

BEDTIME PRAYERS

Prayers at bedtime, packaged in end-of-day conversations, become more than minutes on the clock. A child will frequently pray about what's on their heart. Although even young children quickly learn to use a bedtime prayer as a stalling technique, conversations with God just before falling asleep can reflect a deep level of intimacy.

A tired child might ask you to offer a "made up" prayer. Sometimes, a child prefers the familiarity of a "learned" prayer, like those below, that is repeated together with you each night: it becomes their "amen" to the day. A child who falls asleep with a prayer echoing in their head feels wrapped in the arms of a loving parent and a loving God.

Dear God,
I had such a busy day.
Now I want to stop and say,
"Thank you for the time to play
and for loving me today."
Amen.

Dear God,
As I fall asleep tonight,
wrap me in your love.
Cover me with blessings,
sent from up above.

Dear God,
I ask you now to help me sleep
all through the coming night.
Until the dark is chased away
tomorrow with the light. Amen.

I thank you, God, for people
who showed me love today.
Now bless them for their
kindness and listen while I pray:
[Insert the names of people
who were kind to you today].

I see the moon begin to rise.
It's almost time to close my
eyes.

I want to end today with prayer
to thank you, God, for love and
care.

Watch over me, dear God, I
pray, until there is a brand-new
day. Amen.

Dear God,
My heart is full of thanks to you
for this day that is done.
You kept me safe and healthy,
too. You watched me have
some fun.

Now as I lie down on my bed,
I'm grateful for the love
And blessings that you shared
with me
Today from heav'n above.
Amen.

THE OLD TESTAMENT

THE BEGINNING: THE STORY OF CREATION

Genesis 1:1-2:3

There was absolutely nothing at the beginning of time. Empty. Bare. Nothingness. But then God the Creator got to work, and look what happened!

FAST FACTS

Where was the Garden of Eden?

Wherever it was, it's still on the map! Look for possible locations between the Tigris and Euphrates Rivers (Genesis 2:10-14).

GENESIS 1:1–2:3

Long, long ago there was nothing. No flowers bloomed. No dogs barked. No one sneezed. There was nothing. Then God created the world.

On the first day, God commanded light to shine. And light began to shine. God separated the light from the dark. God called the light *day*, and the darkness *night*. And God saw it was good.

On the second day, God separated the ground from the water. There was a huge space above that God called *sky*. There was morning and evening. And God saw it was good.

On the third day, God commanded plants to grow. Dandelions bloomed. Roses smelled sweet. And God saw it was good.

On the fourth day, God created the lights in the sky. God made the moon to shine at night and the sun to shine during the day. And God saw it was good.

On the fifth day, God created ducks that quack and many birds to soar through the air. God created dolphins that leap and many fish to swim in the water. And God saw it was good.

On the sixth day, God created kittens that purr and puppies that bark. God created lions that roar and monkeys that squeal. And then, God created people. God saw all that was made, and it was very good.

By the seventh day, God had finished creating. This day was special. God blessed the day and then rested. That is how God created the world.

KEY VERSE

In the beginning God created the heavens and the earth. **Genesis 1:1**

TALK ABOUT IT

- Who is the newest baby you've seen?

- What new food would you like to try?

- What do you like about new shoes?

- Is there something you don't like about getting new shoes?

- What is the first thing you hear at the beginning of a new day?

PRAY TOGETHER

Dear God, When I think that you created everything out of nothing, I feel ____. You made the oceans that ____ and the birds that ____. You made the sun that ____ and the stars that ____. Wow, God. Thank you. Amen.

NOTE TO PARENTS

Beginnings ooze with energy. Children can barely contain the excitement that accompanies visiting a new place. Although that enthusiasm doesn't always carry over to sampling a new vegetable, introducing children to new experiences is one of the joys of parenting, for we glimpse the world through fresh eyes.

ADAM AND EVE: THE STORY OF THE GARDEN

Genesis 3

Long ago, a man and a woman stood in a garden. In the middle of the garden was a beautiful tree with big, juicy fruit. "Don't touch that tree," God said. What do you think happened next?

FAST FACTS

Adam lived to be an old man: 930 years (Genesis 2:21-25).

A sneaky snake told the first lie (Genesis 3:4).

GENESIS 3

God created a beautiful world. In a garden called Eden, streams flowed, and trees grew tall and leafy.

God made a man, Adam, and a woman, Eve, to live in the garden. Adam and Eve picked their food right off the trees. They ate plump pears and juicy oranges. God told Adam he could eat from any tree, except the tree in the middle of the garden.

One day, a sneaky snake slithered near Eve. He suggested, "Look at this luscious fruit. Eat this fruit and you will be smart."

Eve said, "That's not right. God said we cannot eat from that tree."

The sneaky snake slithered up the tree in the middle of the garden. He whispered, "Eat from this tree, and you will be as smart as God."

The fruit looked delicious. Reaching out, Eve plucked the fruit off the tree. Then she gave some to Adam. Immediately, Adam and Eve knew that they had made a mistake. They saw they were naked. They sewed together leaves from a tree to cover themselves.

Later that afternoon, a breeze whistled through the garden. When Adam and Eve heard God walking in the garden, they were afraid and hid.

"Where are you?" God called. Adam answered, "When I heard you moving through the garden I was afraid. I knew I was naked, so I hid."

God asked, "How did you know you were naked? Did you eat from that tree in the middle of the garden?" Adam said, "Eve gave me the fruit and I ate it." God then asked Eve, "What have you done?" She said, "That sneaky snake tricked me."

Because they had disobeyed, God sent Adam and Eve away. They could never again live in Eden.

KEY VERSE

I have kept my feet from every evil path so that I might obey your word.
Psalm 119:101

TALK ABOUT IT

- Is there any fruit on your table today?

- Adam and Eve heard God walking in the garden. How did they know it was God coming to see them?

- Things often look more interesting once you've been told not to touch. Why is that?

PRAY TOGETHER

Dear God, Thank you for the tasty food. For vegetables like ____ that are fun to eat and fruit like ____ that tastes so sweet. For veggies that grow underground, like ____, and fruit that grows on trees like ____. Thanks for all of it, God. Amen.

NOTE TO PARENTS

Teaching obedience is a long process. A parent knows that rules keep a child safe, but a child may see those rules as an opportunity to test the limits. Rules should be consistent, but a child tries to push our buttons so we bend the rules. A parent knows that when rules are broken, consequences must follow, but even a primary-age child manages to negotiate lesser punishment.

And yet teaching obedience is one of the most important aspects of parenting. The long-term goal is that a child will respect boundaries. But for that to happen, rules must be clearly communicated, consistent, and developmentally appropriate. The story of Adam and Eve and their disobedience is only the first of many lessons in the Bible that highlight the consequences of breaking rules. But when children understand at an early age they need to be responsible for their own behavior, they have learned a critical life lesson.

WATER, WATER, EVERYWHERE: THE STORY OF NOAH

Genesis 6:5–8:22; 9:12-17

When we say the words *I promise*, that means we intend to do something. You might say, "I promise to walk the dog" or "I promise to make my bed." Long ago, God promised to send a big rain. And God did, because God always keeps promises.

FAST FACTS

Where did the ark end up?

The Bible says on Mount Ararat (Genesis 8:4). And if you can locate that, the world will want to know.

The ark was tall: about as high as a four- or five-story building.

GENESIS 6:5–8:22; 9:12–17

Adam and Eve had children. Their children had children. Their children's children had children. Soon many people lived on the earth. Unfortunately, most of these people made very bad choices.

But there was one old man who worshipped God. His name was Noah. God said to Noah, "I will send a flood that will cover the earth, but I will save you and your family. I will also save two of each animal." God told Noah to build an ark (a very large boat). Then when the big rain arrived, Noah's family and the animals

would have a dry place to live. So Noah started building. Noah spent days, weeks, and even years building the boat.

The ark was finally finished as dark clouds gathered in the sky. Noah invited a pair of each animal into the ark. Two cows walked in. Two snakes slithered past. Two kangaroos hopped inside.

Noah's family came aboard, too. Then Noah shut the door of the big boat. Soon, the rain started. It rained for forty days and forty nights. The whole earth was covered with water.

Finally, the rain stopped. God sent a wind to dry up all the water on the land. All of the animals started to leave the ark. Two koalas walked out. Two snakes slithered past. Two kangaroos hopped onto the dry land.

Noah and his family also left the ark. Noah built an altar to thank God for protection and the promise God kept. Then God made another promise: "I will never again send such a flood."

As a sign of this promise, God created a rainbow and put it in the sky. The rainbow is still a sign of God's promise.

KEY VERSE

Your kingdom is an everlasting kingdom, and your dominion endures through all generations. The Lord is trustworthy in all he promises and faithful in all he does. **Psalm 145:13**

TALK ABOUT IT

- Noah was 600 years old when the flood started.

- Who is the oldest person you know?

- How can you tell when a person is old?

- What is hard for an old person to do?

- What is fun for an old person to do?

- What would you like to ask an old person?

PRAY TOGETHER

Dear God, Thank you for making so many wonderful animals: tiny and huge, wild and tame, slimy and feathery, fishy and ____. Thank you especially for animals I love: ____. Amen.

NOTE TO PARENTS

"But you promised" echoes in our head when we fail to read that extra bedtime story or buy the promised ice-cream cone. A child learns faithfulness as we make and keep our promises. That's why it's important we only make promises we can keep.

God made promises to be faithful to us. That doesn't mean life will be easy. That doesn't mean our child will kick a game-winning goal or easily learn how to read, but God promises to be with us.

When walking with a child, we automatically reach out for their hand. God reaches out to touch us, too, when we face situations that are overwhelming or issues that have no answers. We can count on that, because as we are reminded in the Bible verse for this story, God is faithful and keeps promises.

THE MIXED-UP PEOPLE: THE STORY OF THE TOWER OF BABEL

Genesis 11:1–9

A prideful person attracts attention to themselves. They consider themselves more important than others and want to impress people. In this story, we hear about a group of people who learn there's truth to the statement that "pride goes before a fall."

FAST FACTS

Genesis is the first of thirty-nine books in the Old Testament. Genesis has fifty chapters.

GENESIS 11:1–9

Long after the flood, many people lived on the earth. They were like one huge, diverse family. Some of the people wanted to be famous. They decided to build a city for themselves. Inside it, they planned to build a tall, tall tower. It would be so tall, it would reach into the sky. The people were proud of this idea. They wanted others to say, "Those builders are great."

The people started to work. Brick on top of brick, the tower began to rise. They were proud and pleased. They became famous.

As people watched the tower
rise higher and higher, they said,
"Those builders are great." But
God was not pleased. The people
were so busy feeling great, they
forgot that God was great.

Then people were becoming too
proud of their tower. God said,
"I will confuse them by making
them speak different languages.
Then they will not understand
one another."

The people tried to build. But soon they began to argue among themselves. Everyone was talking, but they could not understand one another. They were all speaking in different languages.

Finally, they stopped building. The builders abandoned the tower. Some of them moved away.

The leftover city was called Babel, which comes from a Hebrew word for *confused*.

KEY VERSE

Pride goes before destruction,
a haughty spirit before a fall.
Proverbs 16:18

TALK ABOUT IT

- Why is a building called a skyscraper?

- What is the tallest building you have been in?

- What are three ways you could get to the top of a tall building?

- If you were in a tall building when the electricity went out, what would you do?

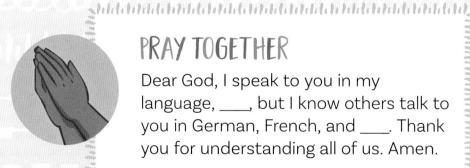

PRAY TOGETHER

Dear God, I speak to you in my language, ___, but I know others talk to you in German, French, and ___. Thank you for understanding all of us. Amen.

NOTE TO PARENTS

As parents, it's sometimes hard to know where to draw the line between honest praise and effusive affirmation. We certainly want children to feel good about themselves; children with a positive self-concept perform better in school and are often happier people. But excessive applause and unearned compliments undermine the sense of trust that is at the heart of every healthy relationship. A child trusts that what we say is true. When we exaggerate the truth, that dishonesty whittles away our solid bond.

We must provide praise tempered by reality. After all, a child thrives when we catch him being good. But we don't need to always prevent a child from making a mistake. When a child is not in danger of hurting themselves or someone else, that child can learn from their mistakes and then move forward. When this happens, a child will bask in the glow of our honest affirmation.

THE TRAVELS OF ABRAM:
THE STORY OF ABRAM

Genesis 12:1-9; 13:1-18

This is a story about Abram, a man who took a very long journey. The only problem was that Abram didn't know where he was going! But that was no problem for Abram. Do you know why? Listen to his story.

FAST FACTS

God spoke to Abram about 400 years after the big flood (Genesis 12:1-8).

Abram built altars wherever he traveled: in Shechem, Hebron, and Moriah (Genesis 12:7-8; 13:18; 22:2, 9).

GENESIS 12:1-9; 13:1-18

Abram was a wealthy man. He lived in a big tent. Abram owned goats, sheep, and cattle, too. He was seventy-five years old when God surprised Abram.

God said, "Leave your country, your home, and your friends. I will show you a new place to live." Abram liked his big home. He liked living near friends and relatives, but Abram obeyed God. He set off with his nephew Lot. They rounded up their goats, sheep, and cattle and waved goodbye to their families.

Abram and Lot didn't know where

they were headed but trusted God's direction. Soon they reached a land that was very crowded with people. When Abram and Lot arrived with their goats, sheep, and cattle, there wasn't enough pasture for all the animals. Lot's shepherds argued with Abram's shepherds. Each wanted the best grazing land for their animals. Finally, Abram said, "We are family. We should not fight like this."

Abram said to Lot, "Look at the land in front of us. If we go in separate directions, there will be space for all the animals. You choose which land you'd like."

Lot looked around. He chose the beautiful valley. Abram was left with the dry desert.

But that night, God spoke to him. "Look around you, Abram, to the north, south, east, and west. I will give you and your family all the land you see. One day you will have as many descendants as stars in the sky."

Abram believed God. He had followed where God led and knew that God would continue to bless his family.

TALK ABOUT IT

- A compass gives directions. There are four major directions on a compass: north, south, east, and west.

- Who might need a compass?

- When would you use a compass?

- Where have you seen a compass?

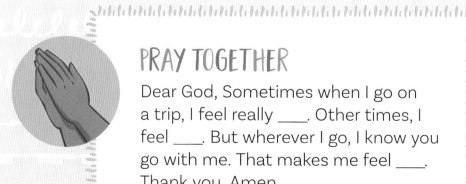

PRAY TOGETHER

Dear God, Sometimes when I go on a trip, I feel really ____. Other times, I feel ____. But wherever I go, I know you go with me. That makes me feel ____. Thank you. Amen.

NOTE TO PARENTS

A child in the primary grades begins to learn about concepts related to time and space. Until this point, a child has been a concrete thinker: she understood what she could see, hear, touch, smell, and feel.

Help your child learn about abstract concepts by inviting her to record the daily outdoor temperature on the calendar. Over time, she will use abstract thinking to draw conclusions about the temperature. For example, as she watches the numbers go up, she might comment, "The temperature is getting warmer every week. Soon I can swim in the pool."

Whenever possible, invite your child to use a compass, thermometer, and calendar. These activities will help your child understand concepts related to time and space.

THE KIND BRIDE:
THE STORY OF REBEKAH

Genesis 24:1-61

There are many ways to show kindness. We can hold open a door for someone who is carrying groceries. We can share a snack or buy a birthday present for a friend. In this story, we learn about Rebekah, who was helpful and kind.

FAST FACTS

A tent was a great place for Rebekah—that is, if you like to sleep under a roof of animal skins.

Rebekah wore the first bridal veil mentioned in the Bible (Genesis 24:65).

GENESIS 24:1-61

Abram (who by now had been given a new name, Abraham) had a son named Isaac. When Isaac was old enough to get married, Abraham told his helper, "Go and find my son a wife."

The helper was worried. "What if I cannot find a bride for Isaac?" he asked. "Or what if I find a bride, but she will not come with me?" Abraham said, "God will send an angel to go in front of you."

Abraham's helper agreed to go. He loaded ten camels with gifts, then started on the journey to find a bride for Isaac. After many long and exhausting days of traveling, the man stopped at a well. He

prayed, "Dear God, please help me find a bride for Isaac. If I ask a woman for a drink, and she also offers to water my camels, I will know she is to be Isaac's wife."

Before the man finished praying, a beautiful woman named Rebekah came to the well. She filled her jug with water. Abraham's helper asked, "May I please have a drink from your jug?" Rebekah kindly poured him a drink.

"Would you like me to water your camels, too?" Rebekah offered. "At my home we have plenty of straw and food for your camels. We also have room for guests."

Her kindness pleased Abraham's helper. He met Rebekah's family and explained the reason for his journey. He told how God had led him to Rebekah. Then he unloaded the gifts from the ten camels.

Rebekah agreed to marry Isaac. So, early the next morning, Rebekah said goodbye to her family and began the long journey to her new home.

KEY VERSE

It is a sin to despise one's neighbor, but blessed is the one who is kind to the needy. **Proverbs 14:21**

TALK ABOUT IT

- What is another word for kindness?

- When has a person been kind to you? How did you feel?

- When have you been kind to someone? How did you feel?

PRAY TOGETHER

Dear God, Many people have been kind to me. I think especially of my friend ___, who ___. Please help me to be kind to others. Amen.

NOTE TO PARENTS

Has your child learned that both sides of kindness feel good? It feels good to be kind. It also feels good to receive kindness.

As social circles expand during the primary years, kindness can be forgotten in the desire to do what peers define as popular. Unfortunately, in some situations and with some children, being unkind can be considered cool. Encourage your child to pause and think before saying or doing something that might be unkind.

Help your child to practice kindness. Invite your child to accept a challenge: you will both promise to be especially kind to at least one person every day. Then at bedtime, share what happened. Soon, the same type of caring modeled by Rebekah in this Bible story will become a natural part of everyday life for you and your child.

THE AMAZING DREAM: THE STORY OF JACOB

Genesis 28:10-22

Dreams are stories or pictures that come into our heads while we sleep, unless of course we're awake. When we are awake and imagine things, that is called daydreaming. Dreams can be good or scary, happy or sad. Long ago, a man named Jacob had an amazing dream.

FAST FACTS

Jacob's pillow was as hard as a rock. Actually, it *was* a rock (Genesis 28:11).

Jacob was the younger twin brother to Esau (Genesis 25:26).

GENESIS 28:10-22

Jacob was a young man in the middle of a very long trip. He walked and walked and walked. By nighttime, Jacob was exhausted. He looked for a place to sleep. He saw only rocky, sandy ground.

So Jacob lay down on the hard ground and used a very big rock for a pillow. He was so tired, he fell fast asleep.

While he slept, Jacob had a wonderful dream. He saw a ladder that reached up to heaven with angels going up and down. And at the very top of the ladder, Jacob saw God.

Then God spoke to Jacob. God promised to be with Jacob wherever he went, to watch over him and protect him.

When Jacob woke up, he remembered his dream. He remembered seeing the ladder and the angels. Jacob knew he had seen the gate to heaven.

He wanted to always remember this place as the house of God, so Jacob made his stone pillow into an altar.

Jacob knew God had been with him in this place. He was certain God would go with him wherever he went.

KEY VERSE

I am with you and will watch over you wherever you go, and I will bring you back to this land. I will not leave you until I have done what I have promised you. **Genesis 28:15**

TALK ABOUT IT

- Fill in the blanks using opposites:

- Jacob was not riding. He was ____.

- Jacob's pillow was not soft. It was ____.

- In his dream, the angels were going up and ____.

- Jacob did not forget his dream. He ____ it.

- Jacob knew God would not leave him alone. God would always ____.

PRAY TOGETHER

Dear God, Sometimes my dreams are scary. Sometimes my dreams are happy, like when ____. If pictures or stories come into my head that are frightening, help me remember that you are always with me. Thanks, God. Amen.

NOTE TO PARENTS

Your child has been learning about opposites since his very first bath: he was wet; you dried him. Since then, he's experienced the contrast between hot and cold, big and little, open and closed. Those early lessons used concrete objects: he could feel cold icicles through warm mittens, roll a big and a small snowball, and hear an open door shut.

Now that your child is older, learning about opposites goes beyond mere word association to include abstract ideas and value judgments: good and bad, true and false, right and wrong. Many of the situations in which your child finds himself will present stark contrasts between these opposites. As a result, much of the teaching you do during these years will provide a framework for your child's choices throughout life.

The story of Jacob teaches us that God is with us all the time, not only when we make the right choices. Like Jacob, your child can view that as a promise, not a threat.

THE JEALOUS BROTHERS:
THE STORY OF JOSEPH'S BROTHERS

Genesis 37:3-4, 12-28

In this story, Joseph had a beautiful coat. But Joseph also had a problem: His brothers were jealous. They wanted his coat. Joseph's brothers were also cruel. Do you know anyone who is jealous? Has anyone ever been cruel to you? If you know people like that, then you know how Joseph felt during this story.

FAST FACTS

Joseph's brothers were jealous of his tunic, a sack-like garment (Genesis 37:3).

The boys didn't fight over Joseph's sandals, which were probably just like theirs: dried grasses woven together and tied with a leather strip.

GENESIS 37:3–4, 12–28

Joseph had a beautiful coat. It was a gift from his father, and Joseph wore his coat everywhere. He wore his coat when taking care of the sheep. He wore his coat when pulling up water from the well. And he snuggled under his coat on cool nights. Joseph's brothers were jealous.

Because Joseph was the only son with a beautiful coat, the brothers hated Joseph.

One day, Joseph's father said, "Go to the fields and see how your brothers are doing." So Joseph wore his

beautiful coat to visit his brothers, who were camping near flocks of sheep and goats.

Joseph was still far away from the camp when his brothers caught a glimpse of that beautiful coat. "When Joseph gets here, let's kill him," they said.

So when Joseph came near, the brothers grabbed him. The mean brothers ripped off the beautiful coat and tore it apart. They ignored Joseph's cries for help and tossed him into a deep hole.

Just then, a group of travelers came riding on camels. The brothers yanked Joseph out of the hole and sold him to the travelers.

The brothers went home with silver money jingling in their pockets. Joseph was dragged off by the travelers.

KEY VERSE

To do what is right and just is more acceptable to the Lord than sacrifice.
Proverbs 21:3

TALK ABOUT IT

- What kind of coat did Joseph wear?

- Why did Joseph's brothers hate him?

- How were the brothers cruel to Joseph?

- Who went home with money jingling in their pockets?

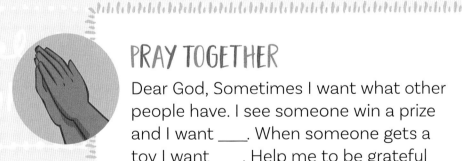

PRAY TOGETHER

Dear God, Sometimes I want what other people have. I see someone win a prize and I want ___. When someone gets a toy I want ___. Help me to be grateful for what I have. Amen.

NOTE TO PARENTS

Children are not the only ones who experience jealousy. Parents can feel envy, too. When other parents host an elaborate birthday party or give their children the newest toys, jealousy can creep into our hearts. We observe jealousy in our own thoughts and feelings; others observe jealousy in our attitude and behavior.

Coping with jealousy includes (1) admitting emotion, (2) dealing honestly with complex feelings, and then (3) moving forward. The next time your child experiences jealousy, help by applying this three-step approach to manage those feelings.

THE LOVING BROTHER:
THE STORY OF JOSEPH

Genesis 41-46; 50:15-21

If you have a mother or father, you have a parent. If you have a brother or sister, you have a sibling. How many siblings do you have? Which of your friends has a sibling? Which of your friends has two siblings? This Bible story is about Joseph and his eleven brothers. That is a lot of siblings!

FAST FACTS

Joseph's brothers looked for food at the palace (Genesis 43:1–2).

There were kisses and tears during Joseph's family reunion (Genesis 45:15).

GENESIS 41-46; 50:15-21

Joseph was hardworking, honest, and trustworthy, and God kept him safe. Eventually, Joseph became a wise ruler who lived in a palace. He wore handsome clothes, but he never forgot his father and his brothers. Joseph also remembered the many ways God had blessed him.

One day, Joseph's brothers came to the palace looking for food. They did not recognize Joseph. After all, it had been many years since they had ripped off their brother's beautiful coat, thrown him into a hole, and sold him.

Although the brothers did not

recognize Joseph, he recognized them. Joseph invited them into the palace for dinner.

The guests all sat. They still did not recognize Joseph.

After the meal, Joseph asked the servants to leave so he could be alone with his guests. Then Joseph said, "I am Joseph, your long-lost brother."

At first, the brothers were shocked. Then they shook with fear. They remembered what had happened long ago. They remembered how mean they had been. Would Joseph now be mean to them?

But Joseph stretched out his arms in welcome. "Don't be afraid," he said. Then he told his brothers about the many ways God had blessed him during the years. Later, the brothers left the palace to go home. Joseph instructed his brothers to return, bringing their father with them. The brothers obeyed.

When Joseph finally saw his elderly father, the mighty ruler cried tears of joy. After a happy reunion, the family lived together for a long time in the land Joseph helped rule.

KEY VERSE

Do not hate a fellow Israelite in your heart. Rebuke your neighbor frankly so you will not share in their guilt.
Leviticus 19:17

TALK ABOUT IT

- An adjective is a word that describes someone or something.

- Words like *smart, short,* and *happy* are examples of adjectives.

- In this Bible story, Joseph was described as hardworking, honest, and trustworthy.

- How would you describe the person who is reading with you now?

- What words describe you?

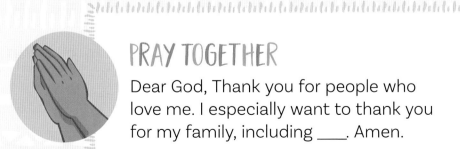

PRAY TOGETHER

Dear God, Thank you for people who love me. I especially want to thank you for my family, including ___. Amen.

NOTE TO PARENTS

It's not easy to forgive and forget. Children must repeatedly experience being forgiven and forgiving others before they begin to embrace the freedom that accompanies both sides of forgiveness.

As parents, we sometimes find it easier to forgive a child than to forgive ourselves. We might remember again and again the day we forgot to pick up a child after baseball practice or punish ourselves repeatedly for a rude remark about a teacher.

To truly forgive and forget, we must ask God for the wisdom to learn from our mistakes and the courage to move ahead with a clear conscience.

BABY IN A BASKET:
THE STORY OF MOSES

Exodus 1:22-2:10

When you were a baby, did you sleep in a cradle? Did you sleep in a crib? Those are safe places for a baby to sleep. In this story, you will hear of a baby who slept in a basket that floated down a river. You will learn why a basket was a good place for this baby.

FAST FACTS

Moses was only three months old when he floated down the river (Exodus 2:2).

Moses' boat was made of grasses woven together and sealed with tar to make the basket waterproof (Exodus 2:3).

EXODUS 1:22–2:10

Miriam loved her new baby brother. He was so tiny! But their mother was worried. The king wanted to steal all the baby boys in the whole country. Miriam and her mother wanted to keep their baby safe. But where could they hide him?

Then Miriam's mother had an idea: They would make a little boat. The baby could safely float down the river, away from the soldiers.

Miriam's mother made a basket and laid the baby inside. Then she put the basket in the river and let it float

away. Miriam crept along the shore, watching through the tall river grass.

When the basket neared the palace, Miriam could hear her baby brother begin to stir and cry. Would the king's soldiers hear the baby, too?

"What is that sound?" asked the princess, bathing in the river. She didn't see Miriam hiding in the grass. The princess waded toward the sound. There, caught in the grass, was the basket. "Ah, a little baby boy," said the princess as she cuddled the crying infant.

Miriam came out from her hiding place. "Would you like me to find someone to nurse the baby?" she said. "That would be wonderful," said the princess.

Miriam raced home to fetch her mother. The princess said, "Take this baby and nurse him for me."

Miriam's mother took the baby home and looked after him until he was big enough to live in the palace. The princess called him Moses, which means *I lifted him out of the water.*

KEY VERSE

The blameless spend their days under the Lord's care, and their inheritance will endure forever. **Psalm 37:18**

TALK ABOUT IT

- Action words are called *verbs*.

- Answer these questions about people's actions in this story:

- Who grew? Who searched? Who hid? What floated? Who cried?

PRAY TOGETHER

Dear God, I know you watched over baby Moses long ago. You are watching over me right now. When I think about how you are right here with me at this very moment, I ___. Thank you, God. Amen.

NOTE TO PARENTS

As parents, we can imagine the desperation of Jochebed, the mother of Moses, as she tried to save her baby. We can also relate to her relief when she was allowed to care for her son. Jochebed realized the privilege of being a parent.

Often, the "specialness" of being a parent gets buried in schedule gridlock or hassles of coping with sibling rivalry or behavior issues. But parenting a child is a genuine privilege. Every day can't be designated Mother's Day or Father's Day, but every day we can thank God for the privilege of being called a parent.

NO, NO, MOSES:
THE STORY OF THE PLAGUES

Exodus 7:1-12:32

Parents often say No to a child's request. Whether a child is begging for another ice-cream cone or the opportunity to stay up late, a parent does what is best for the child. In this story, a ruler says No nine times . . . before he says Yes.

FAST FACTS

Moses was eighty years old when he stood before Pharaoh (Exodus 7:7).

Over 600,000 people left Egypt (Exodus 12:37).

EXODUS 7:1-12:32

Moses loved God. Moses loved God's people. That is why Moses was so sad that God's people had become slaves to an evil pharaoh.

God said to Moses, "Tell the Pharaoh to free my people." So Moses went to the palace. He stood before the ruler and said, "God's people should not be slaves. Let the people go."

But the Pharaoh only made God's people work harder.

God said to Moses, "Return to Pharaoh. Tell him to let my people go."

But Pharaoh would not let the people go. God then sent a plague, or disaster, as a sign of God's power. Moses returned to Pharaoh and again begged him, "Let God's people go."

But the ruler again said, "No, no, Moses."

God sent another plague. This time, God sent frogs to jump everywhere. Frogs jumped in houses, beds, ovens, even in cooking pots.

Pharaoh still did not free the people.

God sent another plague and then another. First it was pesky little bugs, then great swarms of flies.

After each plague, Moses returned to Pharaoh. Each time, when Pharaoh refused to let the people go, God sent another plague.

After nine plagues, God sent one final, terrible plague.

In the middle of the night, Pharaoh called for Moses to come to the palace. Pharaoh said, "Go, go, Moses. Take the people and go." God's people were finally free.

KEY VERSE

The Lord is my strength and my defense; he has become my salvation. He is my God, and I will praise him, my father's God, and I will exalt him.
Exodus 15:2

TALK ABOUT IT

- Pharaoh was the ruler of Egypt.

- Countries can also be ruled by kings, queens, presidents, or prime ministers.

- What is the leader of your country called?

- What is a problem your leader might try to solve?

PRAY TOGETHER

Dear God, I am so grateful I am free to be me. I have the opportunity to ___ and the privilege of ___. As I grow up, I hope I can ___. Thanks, God. Amen.

NOTE TO PARENTS

Children often choose to hear the story of Moses and Pharaoh. Perhaps it's because children delight in the mental picture of frogs jumping in and out of cooking pots or great swarms of flies chasing the cruel Egyptians.

But the underlying theme of freedom is also attractive to independence-seeking children. Yet, as children grow up, they discover more freedom implies more responsibility. The privilege of a later bedtime may mean there's time to fold laundry. Or getting a cell phone may include paying at least some of the cost. Pairing increased freedom with more responsibility as a child grows up is one way to help them learn to balance lifestyle elements.

THE BIG CHASE: THE STORY OF THE JOURNEY OUT OF EGYPT

Exodus 13:17–14:31

Has anyone ever chased you? It can be frightening to try to get away quickly. You might look for a hiding place or run so fast that you finally escape. In this story, Moses and God's people were being chased by 600 chariots. What do you think happened?

FAST FACTS

When God parted the waters of the Red Sea, the people walked on dry land, not the oozy, gooey mud found under a body of water (Exodus 14:22).

EXODUS 13:17-14:31

"Hurry," Moses urged. "We must leave Egypt now." God's people rushed out of their houses. They grabbed whatever they could carry. They desperately wanted to escape from the mean king.

Day and night, God's people traveled, following where Moses led. Finally, the exhausted travelers stopped to camp at the edge of a sea. But God's people couldn't rest because they heard something. Horses thundered in the distance. Six hundred chariots were headed straight toward them. The mean king and his army were chasing them.

Where could God's people go? The sea was in front of them. The mean

king and his warriors were behind them. The people panicked and cried out.

But Moses said calmly, "Don't be afraid. Watch the Lord rescue you today."

Then the Lord told Moses, "Raise your hand over the sea. Divide the water so my people can walk through the middle of the sea on dry ground."

Moses followed God's directions. When Moses raised his hand over the sea, the Lord opened a path through the water with a strong wind. Walls of water stood on either side as God's people surged forward.

When all of the people had walked across the dry path, the Lord told Moses, "Raise your hand over the sea again. Then the waters will rush back and cover the chariots."

Waves crashed with a thundering roar. The dry path disappeared under the water. The soldiers and their chariots were swept away.

God's people were astonished to see God's tremendous power. Their hearts overflowed with gratitude as they thanked God.

KEY VERSE

Who among the gods is like you, Lord?
Who is like you—majestic in holiness,
awesome in glory, working wonders?
Exodus 15:11

TALK ABOUT IT

- God's people in this story experienced many different emotions, or feelings.

- When did the people feel relieved? Exhausted? Fearful? Astonished? Thankful?

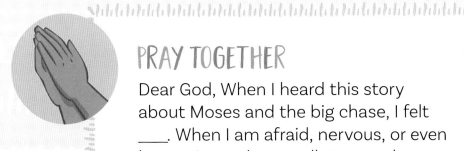

PRAY TOGETHER

Dear God, When I heard this story
about Moses and the big chase, I felt
___. When I am afraid, nervous, or even
happy, I can always talk to you about
my feelings. Thank you for listening to
me. Amen.

NOTE TO PARENTS

As you talked with your child about the various feelings God's people experienced in this lesson, you were helping him build emotional literacy. So often, we slip into speaking patterns when we use the same words repeatedly. For example, at some point today, you might have used the common "feeling words": *happy, angry, sad,* and *tired.*

Helping your child match his feelings more exactly with the correct term expands his emotional vocabulary. This also allows you to more effectively help him cope with the feeling. Next time your child complains, "I'm bored," encourage him to be more specific. Is he tired of playing that computer game? Upset that his friend can't come over? Disappointed that he didn't get a party invitation? Sad that it's raining and he can't play outside? Frustrated that his sister won't share? Accurately identifying an emotion is the first step toward coping.

WHAT IS IT? THE STORY OF FOOD IN THE DESERT

Exodus 15:22-16:36

What do you do when you are tired, hungry, and thirsty? You probably find food to eat and get something to drink. Perhaps you even take a nap so you don't feel crabby. In this story, the people Moses led out of Egypt complained about being tired, hungry, and thirsty. See how God helped them.

FAST FACTS

No one has tasted manna since the Israelites' desert journey (Exodus 16:14–15).

The Israelites wandered in the desert for forty years.

EXODUS 15:22–16:36

Finally God's people were free. They were free from the mean king and free to go to the land God promised them.

But after walking through the desert for three days, the travelers were thirsty. When they finally found water, it tasted terrible.

The people complained, "What are we going to drink?" Moses turned to God for help.

God told Moses to throw a piece of wood into the bitter water. Moses did as God commanded, and the water tasted wonderful. The people were able to continue their journey.

But after a month in the desert, the travelers were hungry. The people complained to Moses, who once again turned to God for help.

That evening, God sent small birds that the people caught, cooked, and ate.

The next morning, God sent dew to cover the ground. The dew melted into thin flakes that looked like frost.

"What is it?" the people asked Moses. He said, "This is the bread that God has given you to eat." It was white and sweet, like crackers with honey.

Every family gathered as much as they needed. The people called this food from heaven *manna* because that means *what is it?*

The people gathered the food every morning. That is how God took care of the people for forty years.

KEY VERSE

Hope in the Lord and keep his way. He will exalt you to inherit the land; when the wicked are destroyed, you will see it. **Psalm 37:34**

TALK ABOUT IT

- How did God take care of the people when they were thirsty?

- In what two ways did God take care of the people when they were hungry?

- In what three ways does God take care of you?

PRAY TOGETHER

Dear God, I appreciate the many ways you care for me. Thank you for giving me healthy food, especially ____. Thank you for something to drink when I am thirsty. Thank you for giving me a place to sleep when I am tired, and thank you for ____. Amen.

NOTE TO PARENTS

The story of food that falls from heaven overflows with vivid pictures. Can you imagine the surprise the Israelites felt when the flakes on the desert floor tasted as sweet as honey?

Manna doesn't fall in our backyard, but God still surprises us. Unexpected blessings are signs of God's grace. What "manna" will God send you today?

SPIES ON THE ROOF: THE STORY OF RAHAB AND THE TWO SPIES

Joshua 2:1-24

When you think of a spy, do you imagine someone carrying a secret weapon under a dark coat? Or a person who sneaks around in the shadows? In this story, you'll read about spies who hide in an unusual place and escape in an unusual way.

FAST FACTS

Rahab lived in a wall house. Cities were surrounded by walls that were so big and broad, houses like Rahab's were built directly into the walls (Joshua 2:15).

JOSHUA 2:1–24

God's people wandered in the desert for many years. They had almost reached the promised land, but the city of Jericho stood in their way.

Joshua, the new leader of God's people, saw the soldiers standing guard. He could not see beyond the high walls and the big gates. Joshua needed to know what was inside the city, so he sent two spies to Jericho. The spies crossed a river, snuck through the big gates, and then crept through the streets until they found a place to stay.

Rahab's house was perfect. From the house, the spies had a good view of the city. And the house was built into the city wall, so they could escape if danger lurked.

To be sure the men were safe, Rahab hid the spies on her roof under bundles of grain. But the king of Jericho had heard rumors that spies had entered his city. The king wanted

to catch the spies. Soldiers knocked at Rahab's door. But they didn't find the spies who were hiding on the roof.

After the soldiers left her house, Rahab tiptoed up the stairs to the roof. Uncovering the men, she whispered, "You must escape while it is still dark." Then Rahab tossed a rope out the window so it landed outside the city walls. "Climb down the rope. Then escape to the hill country," she instructed. "Stay there for three days until the soldiers have stopped looking for you."

The spies dangled from the rope, then slid to the ground. They escaped to the hill country, where they hid for three days. The soldiers searched for three days but returned to Jericho without finding the spies.

Then, just as Rahab had instructed, the spies came out of hiding. The men returned to Joshua and reported everything that had happened.

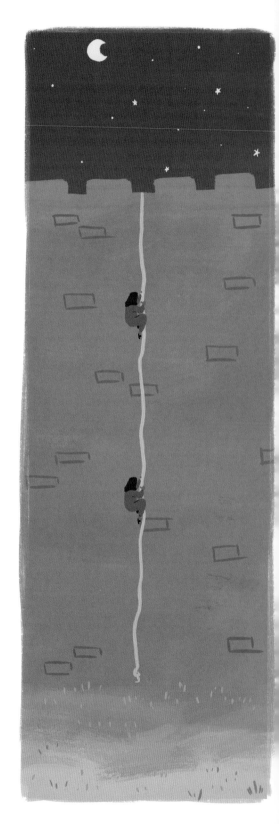

KEY VERSE

In peace I will lie down and sleep, for you alone, Lord, make me dwell in safety. **Psalm 4:8**

TALK ABOUT IT

- What does a spy do?

- Why do people spy on each other?

- If you made a movie of this story, would you make the spies seem like good guys or bad guys?

- Would you like to be a spy?

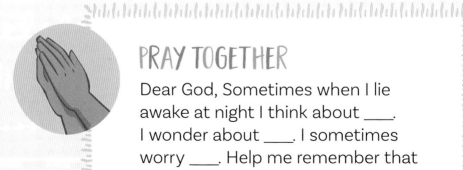

PRAY TOGETHER

Dear God, Sometimes when I lie awake at night I think about ___. I wonder about ___. I sometimes worry ___. Help me remember that you will keep me safe. Amen.

NOTE TO PARENTS

In this story, Rahab and the spies pay attention and follow specific directions. That's good; it's a matter of life and death. Often, the same thing is true for our children. We say, "When you bike, wear a helmet," but sometimes words seem to go in one ear and out the other. To make sure a child hears you, avoid the inevitable miscommunications that result from calling out and not engaging with your child. Instead, look your child in the eye when you have something important to say. Paying attention and following your specific directions could be a matter of life and death.

THE WALLS CAME TUMBLING DOWN: THE STORY OF JERICHO

Joshua 6:1-20

When we talk about God's power, we might remember how God sent forty days and nights of rain in Noah's time. Or we might think of the way God held back the Red Sea so Moses could lead people through on dry land. When God shows power in this story, an entire city collapses.

FAST FACTS

Count aloud: God told Joshua four times to be strong and brave (Joshua 1:6, 7, 9, 18).

JOSHUA 6:1-20

The gates of Jericho were slammed shut and locked. No one could enter or leave. Soldiers stood guard on the high walls.

The Lord told Joshua, "I will help you capture this town. Here's how: March slowly around Jericho once a day for six days. On the seventh day, march slowly around the town seven times. While the priests blast their trumpets, everyone else should shout. The walls will fall down."

Joshua did just as God commanded. On the first day, the priests marched slowly around the city. Then they returned to camp.

On the second day, the priests marched slowly around the city again. Then they returned to camp.

The people did this on the third day, the fourth day, the fifth day, and the sixth day.

On the seventh day, the people got up at daybreak. They marched slowly around Jericho, again and again and again.

The people marched around the town seven times, just as God had commanded.

Then the priests blew their trumpets. A shout went up from God's people. The walls came tumbling down, and Joshua captured Jericho.

Our help is in the name of the Lord, the Maker of heaven and earth.
Psalm 124:8

TALK ABOUT IT

- Ordinal numbers tell the position or indicate the order of something.

- Talk about these everyday situations that use ordinals:

- What is the first thing you do after sitting down to eat?

- What fourth-grader do you know?

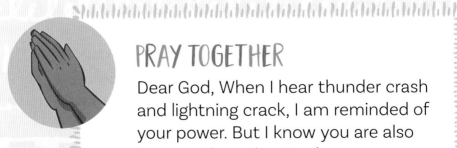

PRAY TOGETHER

Dear God, When I hear thunder crash and lightning crack, I am reminded of your power. But I know you are also very gentle and caring because ___. Thank you, God, for being you. Amen.

NOTE TO PARENTS

Integrating math vocabulary and concepts can boost a child's comprehension and give meaning to academic skills. For example, ask your child to calculate the amount of dry ingredients when doubling a recipe. Or have her use information printed on the map to estimate your time of arrival at Grandma's. As your child relates mathematics to real-life situations, she will understand the importance of measurement, graphs, and numbers.

THE TIMID WARRIOR:
THE STORY OF BARAK AND DEBORAH

Judges 4:4-16

Barak was an army leader. He commanded thousands of soldiers. He should have been brave, but he wasn't. In this story, Barak asks for help to win a big battle. Who do you think helps this hesitant leader?

FAST FACTS

Deborah was the only woman judge in Israel (Judges 4:4).

Mount Tabor, where Barak based his troops, is more than 1,800 feet high (Judges 4:6).

JUDGES 4:4-16

Barak was a leader of God's army. God said Barak should take 10,000 soldiers to fight a battle at Mount Tabor. God promised to help him win, but Barak was timid.

Barak said he would not go alone. He wanted Deborah, a wise judge, to accompany him. He told Deborah, "I'm not going unless you go."

"All right," said Deborah. "I'll go, but you won't get credit for winning the battle."

Barak gathered 10,000 soldiers and went to Mount Tabor. Of course, Deborah also went to the mountain.

Barak, Deborah, and the soldiers in God's army looked down from Mount Tabor. They saw 900 iron chariots and enemy troops crowding around their wicked leader.

Barak and Deborah waited patiently up on Mount Tabor. Finally, God told Deborah it was time to attack, so Barak led his soldiers down the mountain.

During the battle, God confused the enemy troops. The wicked leader jumped out of his iron chariot. Horses pulled the chariots in many different directions so that they crashed into one another. The enemy soldiers didn't know which way to turn.

And just as God promised, even though Barak was timid, his soldiers won the battle. But as Deborah promised, Barak did not get credit for the victory.

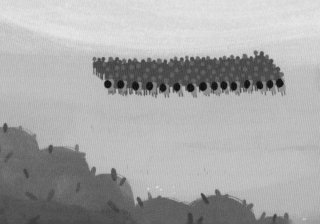

KEY VERSE

"Because he loves me," says the Lord, "I will rescue him; I will protect him, for he acknowledges my name."
Psalm 91:14

TALK ABOUT IT

- In this Bible story, who won the battle?

- Who should get credit for the victory?

- After your sports team loses or you lose a board game, what helps you feel better?

- Some people say, "The best team always wins." Do you agree?

PRAY TOGETHER

Dear God, Sometimes I am brave, like when ___. Sometimes I am hesitant or timid, like when ___. However I feel, I know you will help me. That makes me feel ___. Amen.

NOTE TO PARENTS

We like our kids to be winners. But even encouragement to "do your best" doesn't mean a child always ends up a winner.

Children might actually learn more from losing than they do from winning. We all love to bask in the glow of victory, but we learn patience, perseverance, and other virtues when we aren't number one. We teach some of the most important lessons in those quiet moments when we console a child who didn't win the trophy. Knowing how to learn from losing contributes to making our kids the winners God intends.

THE SHRINKING ARMY: THE STORY OF GIDEON

Judges 7:1–25

Is bigger always better? We might automatically reach for the biggest ice-cream cone or the biggest bag of popcorn. But in this story of an amazing battle, you'll see that bigger is not always better.

FAST FACTS

Gideon was the father of seventy sons (Judges 8:30).

The name Gideon means *great warrior*.

JUDGES 7:1-25

God's people were suffering and begged the Lord for help. So God told Gideon to gather an army. God said, "I will give you the power to rescue my people."

Gideon blew a trumpet to call volunteers. People came from all over, and soon Gideon had a huge army.

But God said, "Gideon, your army is too big. Tell anyone who is afraid to go back home."

And 22,000 people left.

God said, "Gideon, your army is still too big. Take your people to get a drink at the spring. Send home the people who kneel to drink. The

people who lap the water like dogs will be your soldiers."

And 10,000 more people left.

Gideon had only 300 people to battle a huge enemy army. Although he was outnumbered, Gideon believed that God would guide him to victory.

Late at night, Gideon gave each of his soldiers a horn to blow and a clay jar with a torch inside. He said, "Watch me. Then do what I do." Gideon and his tiny army surrounded the enemy camp.

They blew their horns. They broke their clay pots and held the blazing torches in their left hands. Then they shouted, "Fight for the Lord!"

Enemy soldiers rushed around in the darkness. The Lord caused the enemy soldiers to fight each other, not Gideon's soldiers.

After Gideon's tiny army won this fight for the Lord, the people lived in peace for forty years.

KEY VERSE

But I tell you, in this you are not right, for God is greater than any mortal.
Job 33:12

TALK ABOUT IT

- Why is this story titled "The Shrinking Army"?

- What could be a different title for this story?

- How do you think Gideon felt when he watched his army get smaller and smaller?

- Why was Gideon confident he could win the battle with such a small army?

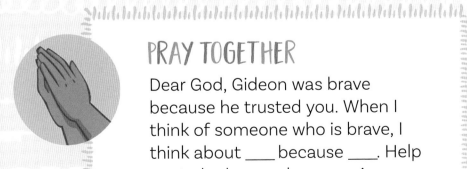

PRAY TOGETHER

Dear God, Gideon was brave because he trusted you. When I think of someone who is brave, I think about ____ because ____. Help me to be brave when ____. Amen.

NOTE TO PARENTS

Each generation of parents faces challenges unique to the historical time frame. Today, you and your child face the invasion of personal space no generation has ever experienced. Unwelcome and unknown guests can reach your child through the computer or cell phone. Thanks to technology, even a child's bedroom is no longer a safe haven.

Like other parents today, you probably use various shields and screens to protect your child. But the best filters are the virtues and values your child carries not in their backpack but within themselves. When your child faces situations, they will repeatedly depend on the beliefs and practices you teach on a daily basis.

Long ago, Gideon and his downsized army faced incredible odds. Sometimes, you might feel like Gideon, who faced a mighty army. Have confidence that just as God defeated the enemy in this story, God can defeat the enemies that threaten you and your child.

THE LOYAL WIDOW:
THE STORY OF RUTH

Ruth 1-4

Loyalty is shown when someone is caring, keeps their word, and stays with their friends and family even when times are tough. In this story, you will learn about Ruth, who stays with her mother-in-law Naomi even when times are very tough. How can you be loyal?

FAST FACTS

Ruth is the first book in the Bible named after a woman.

Ruth was a gleaner, a person who followed the harvesters to pick up what was left on the ground (Ruth 2:2–3).

RUTH 1-4

Naomi was very sad. Her husband had died. Then her sons died. She was left with only her two daughters-in-law, so she decided to move back to her hometown.

During the long journey, she encouraged the women to return to their own families. One kissed Naomi goodbye and left. But the other, Ruth, told Naomi, "I will go where you go. Your God will be my God."

And so Naomi and Ruth kept walking.

They arrived in town at the beginning of the barley harvest. The two women were very poor, so Ruth gathered leftover grain from the field of Boaz, a farmer.

Boaz noticed what a hard worker Ruth was. She followed the harvesters through the fields, picking up every bit of leftover grain. When Boaz learned that Ruth had been so loyal to her mother-in-law, he praised her kindness.

Boaz told his harvesters to purposely drop grain for Ruth to gather. By the end of the day, Ruth had an entire basket of barley.

Boaz invited Ruth to return every day until the end of the season. So Ruth collected grain through the whole harvest.

Boaz was impressed with how hard
she worked. He asked the town leaders
for permission to marry her.

Soon, Boaz and Ruth were married.

And when they had a little baby,
Naomi was no longer sad. She was a
happy grandmother.

Fools mock at making amends for sin, but goodwill is found among the upright. **Proverbs 14:9**

TALK ABOUT IT

- Loyalty is standing up for a friend or family member in trouble.

- How do you show a friend you are loyal?

- What is another word for loyalty?

- Would you be loyal to a friend who asked you to lie?

- When has someone shown loyalty to you?

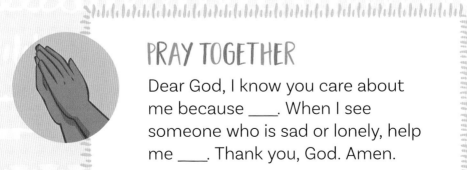

PRAY TOGETHER

Dear God, I know you care about me because ___. When I see someone who is sad or lonely, help me ___. Thank you, God. Amen.

NOTE TO PARENTS

Peer relationships test a child's loyalty. During the next few years, your child will experience different levels of loyalty and learn the meaning of a promise and the cost of being faithful. Some of these lessons will undoubtedly be painful, not only for your child but also for you.

When we see our child hurt by their friends or suffer because of broken promises, we can remember that God alone is always faithful, just like it says in the Bible: "God's love for us is wonderful; God's faithfulness never ends" (Psalm 117:2).

THE POWER OF PRAYER: THE STORY OF HANNAH

1 Samuel 1:2-28

Many things can make us sad. A friend might move away, a bike might be stolen, or we might accidentally hurt someone. At the beginning of this story, Hannah is very sad. At the end of this story, she is joyful. See what happened to Hannah, a woman who prayed faithfully to God.

FAST FACTS

Hannah asked God for a child, so Samuel's name is very descriptive. It means "asked of God" (1 Samuel 1:20).

1 SAMUEL 1:2-28

Hannah loved her husband, and her husband loved her. The couple faithfully worshipped God.

Every year, they left their home and went to the temple to give their offering to God.

But Hannah was miserable. Every year at the temple, another woman teased her.

Once again this year, the woman made fun of Hannah because she did not have a child.

Hannah was so brokenhearted, she couldn't even eat. She went to the

house of the Lord and prayed to God. Her lips moved, but no words came out.

Tears streamed down her cheeks. Hannah's body shook as she cried.

Eli, a priest sitting at the doorpost, looked at the sobbing figure huddled outside the temple. He went to stand beside her and asked, "What is wrong?"

Hannah said, "I am very discouraged. I am pouring out my heart to the Lord. I have been praying because I am so miserable."

Eli reached out to her. Gently he said, "Go in peace. May God grant the request of your heart."

Then Hannah left the house of the Lord. Months later, Hannah gave birth to a son named Samuel.

KEY VERSE

Trust in him at all times, you people; pour out your hearts to him, for God is our refuge. **Psalm 62:8**

TALK ABOUT IT

- Bullies are people who intentionally make fun of others.

- Children can be mean and act like bullies, but some adults, like the woman in this story who tormented Hannah, act like bullies, too.

- Talk about a time you met a bully.

- Do you think all bullies look similar or act the same way?

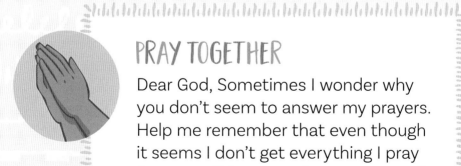

PRAY TOGETHER

Dear God, Sometimes I wonder why you don't seem to answer my prayers. Help me remember that even though it seems I don't get everything I pray for, you still listen. Today I want to tell you ____. Amen.

NOTE TO PARENTS

Bullying can occur in the form of insults, rumors, poking, rejection, gossip, or other behaviors, but prevention is the most effective cure.

Most schools have bullying-prevention programs, but these seldom carry over to extracurricular or out-of-school activities. Bullying is a complex issue, but bullying behavior is not part of healthy child development. Children do not "go through a bullying stage." If you are concerned about the social climate in your child's world, listen attentively as your child talks about peers. Look for changes in your child's approach to an activity or desire to be with specific people. Teach your child social skills. Reassure your child that you are available to listen and support. Both bullies and their victims may need intervention or assistance.

LOST AND FOUND:
THE STORY OF SAUL

1 Samuel 9:1–10:25

When you think of a king, do you imagine a man wearing a jeweled crown sitting on a throne? Some kings look like that. But this story is about a farmer's son who returned to plow the fields after he learned he would be the next king.

FAST FACTS

Saul was the first king of Israel (1 Samuel 10:24).

Donkeys were used to pull plows and carry heavy loads. Travelers put clothes into a basket or small bag, which was tied onto the donkey.

1 SAMUEL 9:1-10:25

A wealthy farmer had a son named Saul. Saul was a tall, good-looking young man who helped his father. One day, their donkeys went missing. Saul and his servant looked everywhere, but they could not find the donkeys.

After searching for three days, Saul's servant said, "Wait a moment. A wise man of God lives in a nearby town. Perhaps he can tell us where to look for the donkeys."

Saul and the servant walked through the city gate and met Samuel, the wise man. God had told Samuel what to say, so Samuel greeted the men and said, "Don't worry about your donkeys. They have been found."

As the two travelers prepared to return home, Samuel said to Saul, "I need to tell you something in private."

After the servant left, Samuel took a small jar of olive oil and poured it on Saul's head. Then Samuel said, "The Lord has chosen you to be the leader of his people."

Then Saul and his servant returned home, but Saul didn't mention that Samuel had anointed him king.

Later, Samuel called together all the people of the land. He announced that Saul, the farmer's son, was the person God had chosen to be their king.

But when the people looked for him, they found Saul hiding behind the baggage! They pulled out the farmer's son so he stood in the middle of the crowd.

Samuel said, "Look closely at the man the Lord has chosen. There is no one like him."

And the crowd shouted, "Long live the king!"

KEY VERSE

"For I know the plans I have for you," declares the Lord, "plans to prosper you and not to harm you, plans to give you hope and a future." **Jeremiah 29:11**

TALK ABOUT IT

- What was lost and found in this story?

- Talk about a time you found something you had lost.

- How did you feel when you found it?

- Talk about a time when you have felt lost.

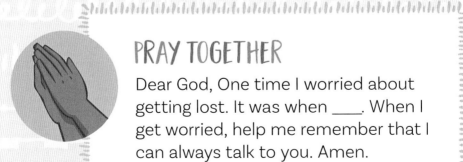

PRAY TOGETHER

Dear God, One time I worried about getting lost. It was when ___. When I get worried, help me remember that I can always talk to you. Amen.

NOTE TO PARENTS

When children are young, one of their greatest fears is that a parent will get lost, although in reality the child is usually the one who is temporarily missing.

Most children will admit the momentary panic they feel when they lose sight of a parent in a busy store or can't find a friend in a new group.

As a child gains life experiences, he discovers he can feel emotionally lost even when in a crowded classroom or at a noisy birthday party. How does your child cope with these times? Talk through scenarios with your child to help him deal more effectively with the panic of being physically lost or the fear of being emotionally alone.

THE SHEPHERD KING: THE STORY OF DAVID

1 Samuel 16:1-13

If you were voting for a new leader, would you choose a person who was tall and good looking, or would you choose someone who smelled like they worked with animals? In this story, you will learn who God chose.

FAST FACTS

David was a man of many talents. He was a shepherd, harpist, warrior, and king. Also a writer, David authored most of the songs in the book of Psalms.

1 SAMUEL 16:1-13

Saul was a good king until he started to disobey God. Then it was time for Samuel to find a new king. God told Samuel, "Go to the town where Jesse lives. I have chosen one of his sons to be the new king. Host a feast and invite Jesse's family to attend." That's exactly what Samuel did.

When Samuel saw Jesse's oldest son, who was tall and handsome, Samuel thought, That must be the son God has chosen. But God told Samuel, "He isn't the one. Some judge by what others look like, but I judge

people by what is in their hearts."

Then Samuel went to Jesse's next son, but God didn't choose him, either. Samuel went to each of Jesse's sons during the banquet, but God did not choose any of the seven boys.

Finally, Samuel asked Jesse, "Do you have any more sons?" Jesse replied, "Yes. My youngest boy, David, is taking care of the sheep."

When David entered the banquet hall, he was dirty and smelly from being in the fields. But as David approached, God told Samuel, "He is the one. Get up and pour the olive oil on his head." Samuel did as God commanded.

The seven boys watched as Samuel anointed their youngest brother and David became the next king for God's people.

KEY VERSE

But the Lord said to Samuel, "Do not consider his appearance or his height, for I have rejected him. The Lord does not look at the things people look at. People look at the outward appearance, but the Lord looks at the heart." **1 Samuel 16:7**

TALK ABOUT IT

- What makes a person attractive?

- Are all famous people attractive?

- Is that important?

- What do people like about you?

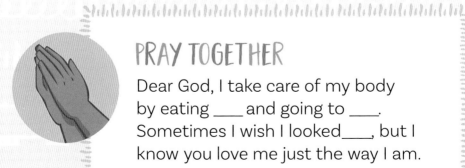

PRAY TOGETHER

Dear God, I take care of my body by eating ____ and going to ____. Sometimes I wish I looked____, but I know you love me just the way I am. That makes me feel ____. Amen.

NOTE TO PARENTS

Samuel assumes that Jesse's oldest son will be king because he is tall and handsome, but God judges what is in someone's heart.

Help your child shift the focus from her external appearance to the skill she's developing. Instead of always complimenting aspects of her physical appearance, look for a way to affirm elements of her character. For example, you might say, "Thanks for setting the table without being asked" or "That was so nice of you to help Aunt Helen get up that big step." Continually reassure your child that it is what is in her heart that matters.

THE SHEPHERD AND THE GIANT: THE STORY OF DAVID AND GOLIATH

1 Samuel 17:1-50

When asked, "Do you have a favorite Bible story?" many people choose this story. After reading about the shepherd and the giant, answer these two questions: Why do you think so many people like this story? Why do you like this story?

FAST FACTS

David is mentioned 1,118 times in the Bible.

Goliath, who was more than nine feet tall, is the tallest man in the Bible (1 Samuel 17:4).

1 SAMUEL 17:1-50

An enemy army gathered to fight King Saul and the Israelites. On the enemy's side was Goliath, a giant who was more than nine feet tall. He wore heavy armor and carried a huge sword.

Before the fight started, Goliath shouted, "I'm the best soldier in our army. Choose your best soldier to fight me."

King Saul and his men heard Goliath, but they were so frightened, they couldn't do anything. Every morning and evening, Goliath came out and challenged King Saul and his soldiers.

One morning, David brought food to his brothers, who were in King Saul's army. David heard Goliath roar his daily challenge. David cringed and said, "The giant shouldn't make fun of God's army."

Then David told King Saul, "I will fight Goliath."

The king was amazed. He asked, "How can you win against a giant?" David responded, "I have protected sheep from lions and bears. The Lord will keep me safe from this giant."

King Saul said, "All right, go and fight him. May the Lord help you."

Then the king gave David his own heavy armor. But David couldn't even walk around in it! So David took off the armor. Instead, he picked up his slingshot and put five smooth rocks into his leather bag. Then David went to meet the giant.

When Goliath saw that David was just a boy, he made fun of him.

David replied, "You've come to fight with a sword and spear, but I come to fight in the name of the Lord All-Powerful. Today, the Lord will help me defeat you."

Goliath took giant-sized steps toward David as David ran toward him. Then David slipped a rock into his sling. He swung the sling around, faster and faster. Suddenly, the rock flew out and hit Goliath. The giant collapsed on the ground. So David killed Goliath without even using a sword!

KEY VERSE

All those gathered here will know that it is not by sword or spear that the Lord saves; for the battle is the Lord's, and he will give all of you into our hands. **1 Samuel 17:47**

TALK ABOUT IT

- Goliath was more than nine feet tall. His chest armor weighed 125 pounds.

- Who is the tallest person in your family?

- Do you weigh more or less than Goliath's chest armor?

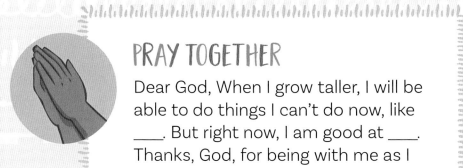

PRAY TOGETHER

Dear God, When I grow taller, I will be able to do things I can't do now, like ___. But right now, I am good at ___. Thanks, God, for being with me as I grow up. Amen.

NOTE TO PARENTS

We all face "Goliaths" in our lives. Sometimes, these problems come and go relatively quickly; other times they last a long time. Regardless of the issue, children watch to see how we solve problems. When the sink is stopped up, do you reach for a plunger? Find a solution online? Bang the sink?

When faced with a child-appropriate issue, share the problem. Discuss possible solutions. Then don't be surprised if the problem-solving technique you used is copied by your understudy.

GOD CARES: THE STORY OF ELIJAH

1 Kings 17:1-16

On the fifth day of creation, God made birds. Some birds have long legs; others sing pretty songs. But God made them all. This story tells how birds helped feed one of God's helpers.

FAST FACTS

Elijah wore a hairy cloak (2 Kings 1:8).

Elijah went to heaven without dying (2 Kings 2:11).

1 KINGS 17:1-16

Ahab was a king who disobeyed God. King Ahab prayed to stone statues and worshipped idols. The one true God was angry, so he sent his prophet Elijah to talk with Ahab. Elijah said to King Ahab, "I am a servant of the one true God. Because you have worshipped idols and forgotten God, no rain will fall on your land."

Then God told Elijah to leave the area and hide near a creek. God said, "You can drink water from the creek and eat the food I've told the birds to bring you." And so every morning and evening, big black birds swooped down from the sky with bread and meat for Elijah. Every day, he cupped his hands to drink sparkling water from the brook. But because there was no rain, soon even the creek dried up.

Then God told Elijah to move to a nearby village, where God told a woman to feed Elijah. When Elijah arrived there, he asked the woman to bring him water and bread.

But she was very poor and barely had enough bread to make supper for her son and herself.

Elijah said, "Make a little bread for me first, then prepare a meal for yourself and your son. God has promised you will have flour and oil in your jars until rain is sent for crops to grow."

Then she went home and baked the bread for Elijah first, then for herself and her son. They ate supper that day, and just as God had promised, they always had food to eat.

KEY VERSE

Trust in the Lord with all your heart and lean not on your own understanding.
Proverbs 3:5

TALK ABOUT IT

- When you are thirsty, what's the first thing you reach for?

- In what ways do you help with food preparation?

- Who do you thank for cooking your food?

PRAY TOGETHER

Dear God, I don't often think about birds except when ___. Hearing this story about Elijah and the big black birds reminded me that ___. I know you took care of Elijah long ago, and I know you care for me today. Thanks, God. Amen.

NOTE TO PARENTS

Is trust the most important virtue you want to teach your child?

Your child started to experience trust within hours after birth: He trusted you would keep him warm, feed him, and care for him. As a preschooler, he trusted you would be at the bottom of the slide to catch him. Now, your child trusts you will arrive to pick him up after choir practice. Trust is about being absolutely, positively certain. Trust is the kind of faith and confidence Elijah showed in this story.

Trust is the foundation of any healthy relationship. Every day, a caring parent demonstrates to their child that "you can trust me." And every day, our loving heavenly Parent wants us to remember that same message.

JARS AND MORE JARS: THE STORY OF ELISHA AND THE WIDOW

2 Kings 4:1-7

We sometimes joke about borrowing a cup of sugar from a neighbor, but in this story, a woman and her sons borrow empty jars. You'll see why they need so many jars.

FAST FACTS

Elisha was plowing a field behind an ox when God called him to serve (1 Kings 19:19).

God led Elisha to perform at least fifteen miracles.

2 KINGS 4:1-7

Elisha loved God and helped many people. One day, a widow told Elisha that a debt collector was going to take away her two sons if she did not pay her bills.

The widow did not have any money. She had only a small bottle of olive oil. Elisha told her, "Maybe I can help. Go around the neighborhood and ask your friends for empty jars. Then go home and fill the jars with oil."

The widow's sons raced from house to house. They asked each neighbor, "May we borrow a jar?"

The boys carried home small jars, big jars, tall jars, short jars, skinny jars, and fat jars.

Finally, there were no more empty jars in the neighborhood; the jars were all jammed into the widow's house.

The boys shut the door.

They watched as their mother carefully poured oil into a neighbor's jar.

She walked from jar to jar, pouring oil from her small jar into the borrowed containers.

Finally, she said to one of her sons, "Bring me another jar," but when the boy looked around, there wasn't a single empty jar left.

Every jar in the house was filled with olive oil. "We don't have any more empty jars," he said.

The widow told Elisha what had happened. Elisha said, "Sell the oil, return the emptied jars, and use some of the money to pay your debts. Use the rest of the money to buy food for you and your sons."

Then Elisha moved on to help other people.

KEY VERSE

In the same way, let your light shine before others, that they may see your good deeds and glorify your Father in heaven. **Matthew 5:16**

TALK ABOUT IT

- Long ago, the oil was pressed out of olives and used to burn in lamps, to cook food, and even to heal cuts and bruises.

- How do you use olives or olive oil?

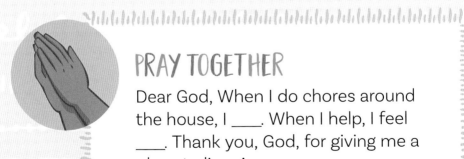

PRAY TOGETHER

Dear God, When I do chores around the house, I ____. When I help, I feel ____. Thank you, God, for giving me a place to live. Amen.

NOTE TO PARENTS

In this story, children scoured the neighborhood trying to find empty containers for their mom. The two boys were driven by hunger, which is a huge motivator, but they were also obedient.

Getting children to help with household chores can appear to be a never-ending battle, and yet children should learn to set the table and make a bed. Those are basic life skills. But helping one's family is another benefit of faithfully doing chores. That type of selfless giving is one sign of a healthy family.

JONAH AND THE BIG FISH: THE STORY OF JONAH

Jonah 1:1-3:3

Fish can swim in an aquarium or an ocean.
Fish can eat bait and tug on a fishing pole.
Fish can be big or small. But can a person live
inside a fish? You'll find out in this story!

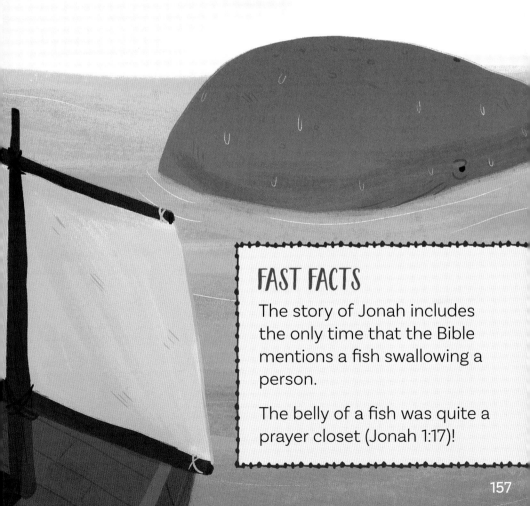

FAST FACTS

The story of Jonah includes
the only time that the Bible
mentions a fish swallowing a
person.

The belly of a fish was quite a
prayer closet (Jonah 1:17)!

JONAH 1:1–3:3

Jonah heard God say, "Go to the city of Nineveh. Tell the people I have seen their terrible sins."

But Jonah didn't listen to God. Instead, he ran from God. He got on a boat that was going in another direction.

After the ship set off, the Lord made a strong wind blow. It tossed the boat from side to side. The storm became so fierce, the sailors threw cargo overboard to lighten the boat so it would not sink. The sailors were so scared, they prayed to their idols.

As the storm raged, Jonah slept below deck. The ship's captain woke

Jonah: "How can you sleep through such a horrid storm? Get up and pray to your God to save us."

The frightened sailors asked Jonah, "Are you the one who brought all this trouble? What should we do with you?"

Jonah said, "Throw me into the sea and the water will calm down. I'm the cause of this terrible storm."

Reluctantly, the sailors threw Jonah overboard, and the sea calmed down. The Lord sent a big fish to swallow Jonah.

Gulp!

While inside the fish, Jonah prayed. He said, "God, you heard my prayer and saved me from the bottom of the sea. Now I will serve you."

After three days and three nights, God commanded the fish to vomit Jonah onto the shore. Once again God told Jonah to go to Nineveh.

This time, Jonah did not board a ship in another direction. This time, Jonah obeyed God and went to the city of Nineveh.

KEY VERSE

Now all has been heard; here is the conclusion of the matter: Fear God and keep his commandments, for this is the duty of all mankind.
Ecclesiastes 12:13

TALK ABOUT IT

- What does it mean to obey?

- Who do you obey?

- Why do parents make rules?

- Who makes the rules that adults obey?

PRAY TOGETHER

Dear God, When I am obedient, I feel good inside because ___. When I don't do what I should, I feel ___. Help me to learn to obey. Amen.

NOTE TO PARENTS

Mercy is defined as an undeserved blessing. In this story, a very undeserving Jonah received God's mercy.

Yet before criticizing Jonah, we must admit we need God's mercy, too. What a blessing that God also gives us more than we deserve. Like Jonah, we fail to listen to God. We repeat the same sins. We continue to make the same mistakes, over and over again.

When we exaggerate the truth, even a little.

When we want to be forgiven but don't forgive others.

When we repeat gossip.

We can say with the psalmist, "You are kind, God! You are always merciful! Please wipe away my sins" (Psalm 51:1).

THE NEW TESTAMENT

THE SURPRISED PRIEST: THE STORY OF ZECHARIAH

Luke 1:5-25

Some people spend their whole life sharing the message of God's love. Some are called pastors, priests, nuns, missionaries, or children's ministers. What are the names of people who have taught you about God?

FAST FACTS

Angels are mentioned 273 times in the Bible.

Zachary, a popular boy's name today, is a form of the priest's name Zechariah.

LUKE 1:5-25

Zechariah had waited all his life for this moment. Some priests never had the privilege, but this very day Zechariah would stand inside the sanctuary at the holy altar.

While a crowd stood outside praying, Zechariah stepped into the sanctuary. Slowly and reverently, he bowed before the altar of the Lord.

Suddenly, an angel appeared next to the altar. The old priest trembled. Shaking and overcome with fear, Zechariah could not speak. He hesitated to even look up. But the angel said gently, "Don't be afraid, Zechariah. You and your wife Elizabeth will have a son. You will name him John. He will be a man of God and will prepare people for the coming of the Lord."

Zechariah could not believe what he was hearing. Shaking his head, the priest asked, "How can I be sure this will happen? Elizabeth and I are very old."

Then the angel said more forcefully, "I am Gabriel. The one true God sent me with this good news. But since you didn't believe me, you will be unable to speak until the child is born."

Meanwhile, the people who had been praying outside the temple were becoming anxious. "What is taking Zechariah so long?" they wondered. "Why doesn't he come out of the sanctuary?"

Finally, Zechariah walked out of the temple, but as the angel had said, he could not speak. The old priest gestured, trying to show with his hands what had happened.

Later, Zechariah returned to his home.

As the angel had promised, Elizabeth became pregnant. She thanked God and waited patiently for the birth of their child.

KEY VERSE

For no word from God will ever fail.
Luke 1:37

TALK ABOUT IT

- In a single day, we can feel many different ways.

- Before breakfast, we are impatient. After stumbling on a stair, we might feel embarrassed.

- When did Zechariah feel joyful? Fearful? Proud? Disbelieving? Excited?

PRAY TOGETHER

Dear God, Thank you for people who teach me about you, like ____. Sometimes when I want to tell someone about you, I feel ____. Please give me the courage and the opportunity to talk about you. Amen.

NOTE TO PARENTS

Parents help children cope with a variety of emotions, but especially their fears. Because a child feels so safe and secure, she often shares her deepest worries with us. In today's world, being alert to what scares a child can help keep her safe.

In the past few years, you have helped your child verbalize fears, sort through them, and cope effectively. However, new fears will continually emerge as situations change and your child moves through different developmental stages.

During times of concern, continue regular routines to give your child a feeling of security. Carefully monitor outside influences, especially technology.

Also, don't wait for your child to approach you. Some children will be hesitant to share their concerns because they don't want to bother us. Remind your child that you are always willing to listen.

VISIT FROM AN ANGEL: THE STORY OF MARY

Luke 1:26-56

Angels are God's messengers. The Bible says there are many angels who sing praises to God. In this story, an angel visits a young woman. As you read this story, ask yourself, "How would I respond if an angel visited me?"

FAST FACTS

In the third chapter of Luke, the family line is traced all the way back to Adam (Luke 3:23-38).

Mary was a young teenager when the angel visited her.

LUKE 1:26-56

A young woman named Mary lived in the town of Nazareth. One day, God sent the angel Gabriel to visit her. The angel said, "The Lord is with you. You are blessed among women."

Mary was confused. She wondered what the angel meant. Then Gabriel told Mary, "Don't be afraid. God is pleased with you. You are going to have a baby. His name will be Jesus."

Mary asked, "How can this be?"

Gabriel answered, "God's power will come over you, so your child will be called the Son of God. Your relative Elizabeth is also going to have a son, even though she is old."

The angel Gabriel continued, "No one thought she could have a baby, but in three months, Elizabeth will have a son. Nothing is impossible with God."

Mary said, "I am the Lord's servant." Then the angel left.

A few days later, Mary went to visit her relative Elizabeth, who lived in the hill country.

Elizabeth told Mary, "God has blessed you, and your child is blessed. You are blessed because you believed that the Lord would do what is promised."

Then Mary sang a song of praise to God. "With all my heart I praise the Lord, and I am glad because of God my Savior. God cares for me. From this day on, all people will say that God has blessed me greatly."

Mary stayed with Elizabeth for three months.

Both women waited with excitement for the day when their babies would be born.

KEY VERSE

And Mary said: "My soul glorifies the Lord and my spirit rejoices in God my Savior." **Luke 1:46–47**

TALK ABOUT IT

- In this story, God sent an angel to visit Mary. What was the name of this angel?

- Use a Bible to find the answers to these questions about angels:

- Who created the angels (Colossians 1:6)?

- What do angels do (Psalm 91:11–12)?

PRAY TOGETHER

Dear God, I know you send your angels to protect me. Thank you for that, God. Thank you also for ____. Amen.

NOTE TO PARENTS

The angel brought a message from God to Mary about an exciting upcoming event.

When we tell children about future events, they can get so excited that it's hard to channel or contain their energy. Even if you're only planning to visit familiar friends or take a day trip, there are new people to meet and things to do.

But the same elements that make an event so interesting to a child can also trigger worries or concerns. A child might miss their pet or regular routines. When approaching special events, and especially when staying away from home overnight, set aside extra time to talk with your child before bedtime.

Praying together, just like you do at home, can be not only a meaningful conversation with God but also an emotional anchor for your child.

A BABY IS BORN:
THE STORY OF JESUS' BIRTH

Luke 2:1-7

In this story of the first Christmas, we learn that Jesus was born in a place where animals were kept. As you read this story, imagine the sounds baby Jesus would have heard. Think about the odors he would have smelled. In what ways was Jesus' birthplace the same as where you were born? How was it different?

FAST FACTS

In the first chapter of Matthew, the writer traces Jesus' family all the way back to Abraham (Matthew 1:1–17).

Mary was a young teenager when the angel visited her.

LUKE 2:1-7

The emperor wanted to know how many people lived in his country. Then he could figure out how much tax money to expect.

So he commanded everyone in the land to return to their hometowns, where everyone could be counted.

Joseph was caring for Mary, who was expecting a baby. Joseph's family was from Bethlehem, so Mary and Joseph were required to travel rom Nazareth

to Bethlehem. It was a long journey.
They traveled for many days. Hour
after hour and day after day, they
plodded toward Bethlehem.

When they finally arrived, the town
was very crowded. Many people had
returned to Bethlehem for the king's
census. So when Joseph tried to find
a place to sleep, no inn had room for
them. He knocked on door after door,
trying to find a place to stay.

One innkeeper felt sorry for the
couple. He could see that Joseph
needed a place for Mary to have a
baby. The man offered, "The only
space in town is where my animals
are kept. I know it doesn't smell very
good, but you will be safe here."

So Joseph settled Mary in for the
night.

While they were there among the
animals, Mary had her baby. She laid
him on a bed of hay in an animal
feeding trough, or manger. And that's
how baby Jesus was born.

KEY VERSE

A child has been born for us. **Isaiah 9:6**

TALK ABOUT IT

- What do you look forward to the most at Christmas?

- In what three ways was the first Christmas different from your last Christmas?

- How do you think Joseph felt when the innkeeper offered him a room with his animals?

- How do you think Mary felt on the first Christmas?

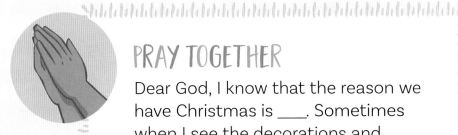

PRAY TOGETHER

Dear God, I know that the reason we have Christmas is ___. Sometimes when I see the decorations and presents, I ___. Help me remember what Christmas means. Amen.

NOTE TO PARENTS

"Keep it simple" sounds like a good idea before each holiday season, but somehow that rarely happens.

And yet the first Christmas really was very simple: a mother, a baby, and someone to care for both. How ironic that this stripped-down scene would become the centerpiece for the biggest commercial holiday of the year.

But too often, the birth of Jesus isn't the focal point. Too often, it's the trimmings that shift our attention away from the reason we celebrate.

The message today is as uncomplicated as the simple setting on that first Christmas: Jesus the Savior is born. Wherever today falls in the calendar year, what are three concrete steps you can take to help your family focus on that central message next Christmas?

A HEAVENLY CHOIR:
THE STORY OF THE SHEPHERDS

Luke 2:8-20

The sounds of Christmas include many familiar songs. At the first Christmas, angels sang, "Glory to God in the highest." Which carol that we sing today includes some of those words?

FAST FACTS

The work of angels is to praise God in heaven. (Hebrews 1:6)

On earth their job is to act as God's messengers, and to protect God's people (Psalm 91:11).

LUKE 2:8-20

On the night that Jesus was born, stars shone in the sky above Bethlehem. Outside of town, shepherds guarded their flocks on the hillside. It was a night like any other night, with the only sound a gentle cry as a lamb looked for its mother.

Suddenly, the silence was shattered. An angel of the Lord appeared to the shepherds. They were terrified, but the angel said, "Don't be afraid. I bring good news. The Savior you have been waiting for has been born in Bethlehem. You will recognize him by this sign: You will find the baby wrapped in cloths and lying in a manger."

Immediately, a choir of angels appeared above the shepherds.

Songs of praise and thanksgiving to God filled the sky as the angels sang, "Glory to God in the highest."

The shepherds were amazed at the sight. They listened with wonderment.

After the angels left and returned to heaven, the shepherds talked among themselves. They said, "Let's go to Bethlehem and see what has happened."

The shepherds hurried into the village. They went from place to place, looking for what the angel had described. Finally, they found Mary and Joseph among the animals. And just as the angel had told them, there was the baby, lying in a manger.

When the shepherds finally went back to their flocks on the hills, stars shone in the sky.

It looked like any other night, but the world had changed forever, for Jesus the Savior was born.

KEY VERSE

This very day in King David's hometown a Savior was born for you. He is Christ the Lord. **2:10–11**

TALK ABOUT IT

- Lots of things were said on that first Christmas night.

- Who might have said these things and what/who were they talking about?

"I'm afraid."
"It smells in here."
"Let's hurry."
"Praise God."

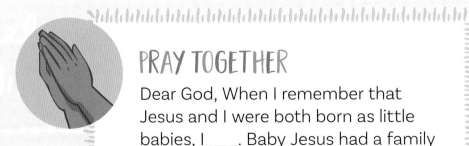

PRAY TOGETHER

Dear God, When I remember that Jesus and I were both born as little babies, I ___. Baby Jesus had a family who loved him, too. Thank you for people who love me, especially ___. Amen.

NOTE TO PARENTS

Angels are often associated with the special gift of singing. As parents, we want to help our children discover and develop their own God-given talents and abilities. Often, that includes several years of nonstop games, practices, recitals, and programs. As children begin to focus on areas of strength and special interest, the schedule becomes more limited in focus but intense in commitment.

During the process of activity elimination, parents are sometimes tempted to project their personal agenda on their child's choices. This often happens out of a sincere desire to help our child find happiness. After all, if a parent gets joy from playing the piano, they might want their child to enjoy music.

Our intentions may be admirable, but children must be allowed to make their own choices. Our role is to nurture skill development, support a child's choices, and celebrate their growing independence.

A STAR FOR THE KING:
THE STORY OF THE WISE MEN

Matthew 2:1-12

Although this story is about a baby, a star, and some travelers, you will also hear about a sneaky king. This ruler tried to trick the travelers. Has anyone ever tried to trick or tease you? How did that make you feel?

FAST FACTS

To get across the desert, travelers rode camels, which could go for up to two weeks without drinking water. Camels are sometimes called called the trucks or ships of the desert.

MATTHEW 2:1-13

The astronomers were growing weary. Their caravan had been traveling for days, following the star of the newborn king.

The camels strode across the rocky desert with long, jerky steps and moved closer to the land beneath the star.

When the caravan neared the big city, the astronomers stopped at the palace for directions.

"Where is the child born to be king of the Jews? We have followed his star and have come to worship him," the wise men explained.

Soon the city was buzzing with word of a new king.

King Herod was not pleased to hear about a new ruler, and called together his leaders.

"Where will this new king be born?" he demanded of his priests and scribes.

They responded, "In Bethlehem."

King Herod pondered this news. Then he secretly told them, "Let me know when you find this child. I want to worship him, too."

Leaving King Herod, the astronomers continued their journey. They traveled until the star stopped above the house in Bethlehem where baby Jesus stayed with his family.

There, the men bowed before Jesus. They knelt and worshipped him. They gave Jesus the treasures they had carried from the East, gold and gifts of expensive fragrances and oils.

The wise men were warned in a dream not to return to King Herod, so they took another route home.

KEY VERSE

Those people who are led by God's Spirit are his children. **Romans 8:14**

TALK ABOUT IT

- The wise men who visited Jesus were astronomers.

- What are two facts you know about astronomers?

- What is one of the newest discoveries an astronomer has made?

- What would be rewarding (or difficult) about working in astronomy?

PRAY TOGETHER

Dear God, Thank you for guiding the wise men to stay away from the sneaky king. When people try to trick or tease me, help me ____. And if I ever feel like being mean to someone, please ____. Amen.

NOTE TO PARENTS

Choice mentality has been embraced as a cultural value, so we teach children how to make choices from an early age. We even let a toddler choose to wear a red shirt or a green shirt.

As children grow up, choices get more complicated. Outside influences, including peers and media, can influence a child's thinking. A child comes to realize that some situations only offer a basic choice between right and wrong. However, to make this distinction, children need a strong moral compass. Otherwise, they can float in a sea of uncertainty as they attempt to distinguish between good, maybe acceptable, or acceptable only in certain situations, and then rationalize their decision.

In the story of the wise men who visited Jesus, the travelers chose to follow God's redirected route for their journey home. Pray today that your child will follow God's direction in our world of choice.

PREPARE THE WAY FOR THE LORD: THE STORY OF JOHN THE BAPTIST

Matthew 3:1-17

This is a story about Jesus' cousin, John. We don't know how many cousins Jesus had, but we know his cousin John helped people learn about Jesus. Do you have any cousins? What do you like to do with relatives who come to visit?

FAST FACTS

John dressed in clothes made of scratchy camel hair (Matthew 3:4).

John ate locusts—boiled, fried, or dried—for lunch and supper. He added honey, too. Yum, yum!

MATTHEW 3:1-17

John was God's servant. He dressed differently than most people: He wore scratchy clothes made from camel hair and tied a leather belt around his waist.

John lived alone in the hot, dry wilderness, where he ate grasshoppers and wild honey.

But crowds came from all over to hear him preach about God.

John's voice could be heard across the barren desert. "Prepare the way for the Lord," he said. "Repent of your sins." Some of those who heard John preach were sorry they had disobeyed God.

John baptized those people in the river. This washing in the water showed everyone that God had forgiven their sins.

After their baptism, these people could have a fresh, clean start in life.

Crowds continued to push forward to hear John. He preached, "Prepare the way for the Lord. One who is coming is greater than I."

And one day, he came. Jesus was the one about whom John preached.

When Jesus reached the river, he waded in to be baptized.

As he stepped out of the water, a voice from Heaven said, "This is My beloved son, who brings Me great joy."

KEY VERSE

Only God can forgive sins. **Mark 2:7**

TALK ABOUT IT

- Antonyms are opposites.

- For example, slow is an antonym for fast. Wet is an antonym for dry.

- Name antonyms for these words that appeared in this story:

Dry, scratchy, desert, plush, disobey, clean, joy, deep, start

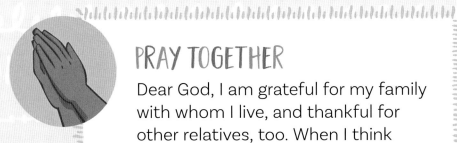

PRAY TOGETHER

Dear God, I am grateful for my family with whom I live, and thankful for other relatives, too. When I think about all the people who love me, I feel ____. Thank you, God. Amen.

NOTE TO PARENTS

A young child often disobeys by doing the opposite of what we ask. But when a child gets older, instead of a flat no, an eight- to ten-year-old will change the subject, bargain, or whine, "It's not fair." Children use their growing cognitive skills to negotiate or wheedle out of a request.

Many parents use contracts for specific chores. A contract identifies a single task, plus it includes a time frame, description of the work to be done, consequence if the job is not done, and reward for a job well done. When this information is written and agreed to, both parent and child often view this as a fair approach.

JESUS TEACHES: THE STORY OF PEOPLE LEARNING ABOUT GOD

Matthew 4:18-5:16

In this story, you will learn that Jesus played follow the leader. Jesus was the leader, of course. But "follow the leader" was more than a game to Jesus. He asked people to join him in telling others about God. In what ways do you let people know that you follow Jesus?

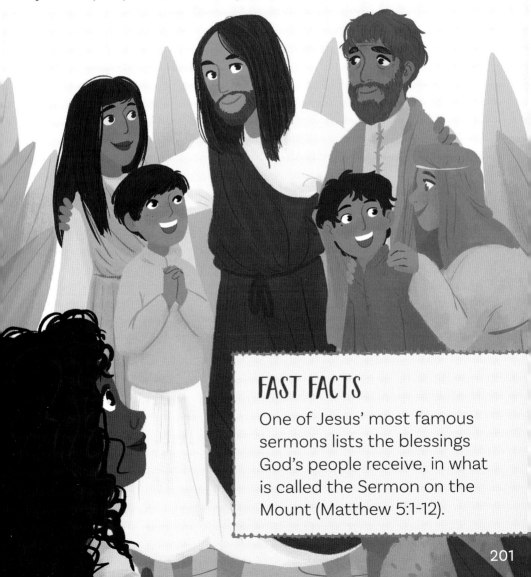

FAST FACTS

One of Jesus' most famous sermons lists the blessings God's people receive, in what is called the Sermon on the Mount (Matthew 5:1-12).

MATTHEW 4:18-5:16

Jesus grew up in the town of Nazareth. He helped his stepfather, who was a carpenter. Jesus worshipped in the temple with his family and even taught some of the church leaders. The men were surprised that, as a young man, Jesus was so wise. Now that Jesus was a grown man, he preached about God all the time.

One day, while he was walking along the shores of a lake, he saw two brothers fishing. Peter and Andrew were tossing their big, heavy nets into the water.

Jesus called, "Come with me. I will teach you how to fish for people."

Peter and Andrew immediately dropped their nets and followed Jesus.

Jesus traveled throughout the land, teaching in the synagogues. Everywhere he went, he preached about God's kingdom. He healed many people, even those who were very sick. Soon people followed Jesus wherever he went.

One day, when Jesus saw the crowds, he climbed up the side of a mountain and sat down to teach.

The crowd listened as Jesus talked about the many ways God blesses those who love God.

Jesus told his helpers that because they loved God, "You are the light of the world."

Jesus encouraged the people to shine by serving, so that others would see their good works and praise God.

KEY VERSE

Jesus said, "Come with me!"
Matthew 4:19

TALK ABOUT IT

- Follow the leader is a popular game.

- When you play this game, do you prefer to be the leader or a follower? Why?

- Parents, teachers, and pastors are some of the people who lead when we aren't playing games.

- What makes someone a good leader?

- Does the most popular person make the best leader?

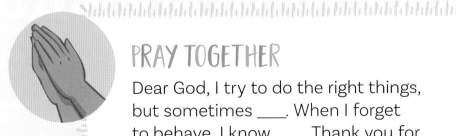

PRAY TOGETHER

Dear God, I try to do the right things, but sometimes ____. When I forget to behave, I know ____. Thank you for forgiving me. Help me to do a better job of following you. Amen.

NOTE TO PARENTS

When asked, "Do you want your child to grow up to be a leader or a follower?" most parents answer, "Leader." That response is understandable, because leaders earn our loyalty and applause.

Although we encourage children to develop character traits that will make them effective leaders, we must also help children to be faithful followers. Every child should learn to listen to directions, show respect to a leader, and support a team effort. These are benefits a child can gain from participating in organized sports, music, drama, and other activities.

What signs have you observed that your child is growing as both a leader and a follower?

THE SOWER AND THE SEED: THE STORY OF THE FARMER

Matthew 13:1-23

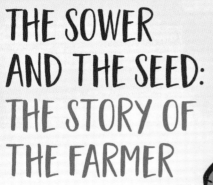

Do you understand everything in the Bible? As you'll see in this story, even people who learned from Jesus himself didn't understand everything he taught.

FAST FACTS

This story is one of only five parables recorded in three Gospels: Matthew 13:1-9, 18-23; Mark 4:1-20; Luke 8:4-15.

MATTHEW 13:1-23

Crowds continued to follow Jesus everywhere he went. One day, there were so many people on the beach where Jesus was teaching, he spoke from a boat so everyone could see him.

Here is a story Jesus told that day: "A farmer scattered his seeds. Some fell on a worn path. Birds swooped down and ate the seeds. Other seeds fell among the rocks. Those seeds grew quickly, but because the plants did not have deep roots, they died.

"Still other seeds fell among weeds. The weeds crowded out the good seeds.

"But a few seeds fell on good ground. These seeds produced a big crop."

When Jesus finished this story, some of his disciples looked puzzled. Others complained and said, "We don't understand what that story means."

So Jesus explained. He said, "The seed is God's message. Many people hear the Word of God, but they respond in different ways. Like the seeds that fall on the hard path, some people have hard hearts and don't believe God's Word.

"Other people are like the seeds that fall on rocky ground. These people only believe in God when it's convenient.

"The seeds that fall among the weeds are like people who are too busy for God. But the seeds that fall on good soil and grow are like people who hear and obey God's word."

After Jesus explained this story, he continued to teach the people.

KEY VERSE

God has blessed you, because your eyes can see and your ears can hear!
Luke 1:37

TALK ABOUT IT

- During Bible times, a farmer planted a crop by scattering seeds with their hands.

- What different types of machinery do farmers use today to plant and tend their crops?

- What would be hard about being a farmer?

- What benefits do farmers enjoy?

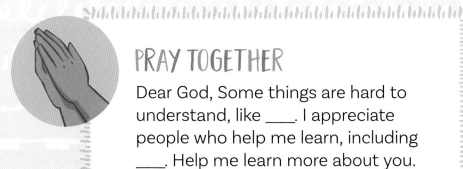

PRAY TOGETHER

Dear God, Some things are hard to understand, like ___. I appreciate people who help me learn, including ___. Help me learn more about you. Amen.

NOTE TO PARENTS

As parents, we sow the seeds of godly character for our children. We hope and pray our model of truthfulness, kindness, and other virtues will "take root." Our actions are important, because a child watches intently how an abstract concept is defined through our everyday activities.

During the early years, a child will automatically adopt many of the virtues she sees modeled and affirmed by the most important people in his life. As a child grows up, she may test these concepts for herself. She may try out actions that show she is wondering, "What if I'm only honest sometimes?" and "Are there some times when honesty isn't the best policy?" But even during the seasons of backsliding, we are like that faithful farmer who returns to the field each spring, continuing to sow the seeds of virtues from which godly character will eventually grow.

THROUGH THE ROOF: THE STORY OF THE PARALYZED MAN

Luke 5:17-26

Friendship and creativity go together in this story. Some men want to help their friend, but they need to come up with a very imaginative solution.

FAST FACTS

In biblical times, people roof-hopped: You could walk from house to house on rooftops. And to eat or sleep on the roof, people climbed stairs that were built outside the house.

LUKE 5:17-26

Jesus preached throughout the area. People came from all over to hear him talk about the kingdom of God.

Jesus also continued to heal people. Those who were sick or crippled crowded around him, eager for his healing touch.

One day, so many squeezed into the house where Jesus was teaching that there wasn't even standing room left in front of the door.

Some men carried a paralyzed man on a sleeping mat. The men wanted

Jesus to heal their friend, but the crowd was so large, the men couldn't reach the door.

So, very carefully, the men carried their friend up the stairs to the flat roof. Then they removed some of the roof tiles so they could see directly into the room below.

They tied ropes onto the sleeping mat and cautiously lowered their friend through the roof. The man landed in the middle of the crowd, right in front of Jesus.

Jesus looked up and saw the faithful friends. Then he looked at the paralyzed man and said, "Stand up, pick up your mat, and go home!"

Everyone watched as, almost immediately, the man jumped up. He picked up his mat and went home praising God.

Those in the crowd also thanked and praised God. They left the house, saying, "We have seen amazing things today."

KEY VERSE

We should help people whenever we can. **Galatians 6:10**

TALK ABOUT IT

- When you say, "You're a good friend," what do you mean by that?

- What is the best part of having a friend?

- What is the best part of being a friend?

- When is it hard to be a good friend?

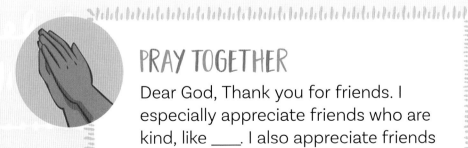

PRAY TOGETHER

Dear God, Thank you for friends. I especially appreciate friends who are kind, like ___. I also appreciate friends who make me laugh, like ___. Thank you for the gift of good friends. Amen.

NOTE TO PARENTS

Compassion is a virtue that seems to disappear among some older children. That three-year-old who rescued drowning earthworms from every rain puddle years later is transformed into a child who appears to have forgotten how to be kind to anyone, especially to family and friends.

Some of this lack of compassion can be attributed to developmental issues. Preadolescents might feel very isolated, becoming so self-focused that they will rarely initiate compassionate acts toward others. And yet, when they are given the opportunity to show kindness, it can propel them beyond their personal pity party.

What situations can be structured to encourage your child to reach out to others? Activities that trigger your child to show kindness will help even the most self-centered preadolescent experience the joy that comes with helping others.

JESUS HEALS: THE STORY OF BARTIMAEUS

Mark 10:46–52

It's hard to see in the dark. We might stumble or reach for something that feels familiar. This story is about a man who lived in the dark. At least he did until he met Jesus.

FAST FACTS

Luke recorded Jesus reading an Old Testament passage that said healing the blind was one of the purposes of his ministry (Luke 4:18).

MARK 10:46–52

After teaching in the town of Jericho,
Jesus and his helpers left the city. A
huge crowd followed. People shouted
and shoved as they attempted to get
close to Jesus. Those sitting along
the roadside were pushed aside.

A beggar, Bartimaeus, heard that
commotion. He was blind.

"What's going on?" asked Bartimaeus.

No one answered, but he overheard
the name "Jesus."

Bartimaeus believed that Jesus was the Son of God, and so he called, "Jesus, have pity on me." But the noise of the crowd drowned out his cry for help.

Bartimaeus called louder, "Jesus, help me."

Some in the crowd warned him to be quiet, but that made Bartimaeus call even louder. Again and again he begged, "Jesus, help me."

Finally, Jesus heard that repeated plea above the commotion and commanded that Bartimaeus be brought to him. Bartimaeus could not see what was happening, so someone told him to get up.

Flinging aside his cloak, Bartimaeus was guided to Jesus, who asked, "What do you want me to do for you?"

Bartimaeus answered, "Lord, I want to see."

Jesus said to him, "Go on your way. Because you believe in me, your faith has made you well."

Immediately, Bartimaeus received his sight.

He looked at Jesus and followed him down the road.

KEY VERSE

As Scripture says, "Anyone who believes in him will never be put to shame." **Romans 10:11**

TALK ABOUT IT

Are these statements true or false?

- Bartimaeus saw the crowd and knew Jesus was coming.

- People followed Jesus wherever he went.

- Jesus healed Bartimaeus because he called so loudly.

- Bartimaeus believed that Jesus was the Son of God.

PRAY TOGETHER

Dear God, Thank you for creating such a colorful world. For the blue ___ and the green ___, the yellow ___, and the multicolored ___, thank you, God. Amen.

NOTE TO PARENTS

The moral compass, which forms the basis for ethical behavior, has shifted. We see the signs of this shift in business, government, and everyday situations.

Distinguishing between right and wrong forms the basis of a child's conscience. Their conscience becomes a testing ground for determining how to behave. Today, there is a growing "gray" area between the two extremes of right and wrong. As a result, a child is challenged when faced with situations that require the application of everyday ethics. For example, your child might wonder, "Should we donate to a beggar? He might use that money to buy drugs." Or, "If a classmate texts me a homework answer, is that considered cheating? I didn't copy his answer."

When wise choices are consistently affirmed, a child's conscience will serve as a dependable moral guide regardless of how the societal landscape changes.

BUILDING A HOUSE: THE WISE AND FOOLISH BUILDERS

Matthew 7:24–27

Jesus often included stories in his preaching. He also talked about real-life things that people recognized, like houses and storms. Jesus knew that listeners who could picture familiar objects in their minds would more easily remember the important points of a story.

FAST FACTS

Buildings in this high-risk earthquake region needed a strong foundation.

This is the last story in the longest sermon Jesus preaches in Matthew, the Sermon on the Mount.

MATTHEW 7:24–27

One day, Jesus preached a long sermon about how people should live. Before Jesus finished talking, he told one last story:

"Two men wanted to build new houses. The first builder was wise. He knew a strong foundation was important, so he searched all over to find a solid piece of ground. He looked until he located land with rock beneath the soil. That's where he built his house. After his house was completed, bad weather came. There was so much rain, the rivers flooded. There was so much wind, it whipped and whistled around the house. But the house stood strong because it was built on solid rock.

"The second builder was foolish. He picked a pretty location but didn't consider what was underneath the soil. Soon after he built his house, bad weather came. Rain poured down, and the rivers spilled over their banks. The wind howled, and the house shook. Then the house collapsed with a crash."

When Jesus finished telling this story, he reminded his helpers to be like the wise builder.

He said, "Be like the smart carpenter who builds his house on a rock foundation. When a storm comes, his house won't fall down. In the same way, if you follow the lessons I'm teaching, you will be able to cope when trouble comes in your life.

"The foolish carpenter builds his house on sand that shifts in rain and wind. When a storm comes, his house will fall down."

After listening to Jesus, the people realized that he was a great teacher who helped them learn about God.

KEY VERSE

Therefore everyone who hears these words of mine and puts them into practice is like a wise man who built his house on the rock. **Matthew 7:24**

TALK ABOUT IT

- Is a person who attends church, reads the Bible, and prays to God more like the wise builder or the foolish builder? Why?

- Who do you know who is like the wise builder? The foolish builder?

- In what ways are you like the wise builder?

PRAY TOGETHER

Dear God, Thank you for people who teach me about you so I have a strong foundation. Thank you for ____ and ____. Amen.

NOTE TO PARENTS

Jesus often illustrated important points by telling parables, earthly stories with a heavenly meaning. This story about the builders is one of these parables.

Until the age of seven or eight, children have not developed the mental skills to relate an earthly story to the heavenly meaning because this requires abstract thinking. This is the reason Bible storybooks for younger children highlight lessons based on concrete thinking and rarely contain parables like this story.

An older child is now able to do some mental gymnastics: they can understand the meaning of this parable and apply it to their life. The way in which a child answers the questions posed after this story will give you clues about your child's level of mental development.

During everyday activities, you can also watch for signs that indicate your child is developing more advanced cognitive abilities. For example, if you ask, "How do you think Matt will feel if he's not invited to the game?" an older child will be able to mentally project how a friend might respond. To do this, a child applies almost adult-level logic, a clear sign that they are using advanced thought processes.

BE STILL: THE STORY OF THE STORM

Mark 4:35–41

Do you hide somewhere when lightning flashes and thunder booms? A bad storm can be scary. Jesus' friends, the disciples, were afraid when they were caught in a bad storm. It was fortunate that Jesus was with them. Read on to hear how Jesus helped!

FAST FACTS

The Sea of Galilee is actually a lake surrounded by mountains.

Violent storms erupt over the Sea of Galilee when cold wind from the mountains meets the warm lake air.

MARK 4:35–41

Jesus had been teaching all day.
Crowds had gathered along the
lakeshore to hear him. In the evening,
Jesus suggested, "Let's go across
the lake." So his friends launched
the boat, and they headed for open
water.

Jesus was tired after the long day. He
laid his head on a pillow at the back
of the boat and promptly fell asleep.

While Jesus slept, a storm brewed over the lake. The wind started to blow, and the boat was tossed about. Waves crashed and splashed over the sides of the boat, filling it with water. Even though the disciples bailed feverishly, the boat was in danger of sinking.

The disciples, fearing for their lives, woke the sleeping Jesus.

"Master, save us!" they begged. "We will drown!"

Jesus asked, "Why are you so afraid? Where is your faith?"

Jesus stood in the middle of the raging storm and said, "Stop, wind."

And the wind quieted.

He said to the sea, "Peace, be still."
And the waters calmed.

The people in the boat were amazed.
In astonishment, they asked, "Who is
this, that even the wind and the sea
obey him?"

People marveled at everything Jesus
did.

KEY VERSE

Everyone who calls on the name of the Lord will be saved. **Romans 10:13**

TALK ABOUT IT

- There were many problems in this story. How were they solved?

- Jesus was tired. What did he do?

- The boat was sinking. What did the disciples do?

- Jesus stood up in the storm. What did he do?

PRAY TOGETHER

Dear God, Sometimes I am afraid. When the lightning flashes, I ___. When the thunder booms, I ___. I also get scared ___. Help me remember you are always with me. Amen.

NOTE TO PARENTS

Every child faces problems. However, children do not always see solutions. Teaching children problem-solving skills empowers them to cope.

Young children can learn a simple, three-step problem-solving technique that is effective even for adults:

1. Stop.
2. Think.
3. Act.

This sounds easy, except that parents usually work backward! As a result, we often respond to a situation before we stop and think.

The next time you or your child faces a problem, try this approach, beginning with step one.

A HUNGRY CROWD: THE STORY OF THE FEEDING OF THE 5,000

Mark 6:30–44

"Hungry, hungry, I am hungry!" Do you ever say those words? Thousands of people were hungry when Jesus was teaching one day. Although there wasn't a store or restaurant nearby, Jesus made sure that no one went away hungry.

FAST FACTS

This is the only miracle of Jesus that is recorded in all four Gospels (Matthew 14:13–21; Mark 6:30–44; Luke 9:10–17; John 6:1–13).

MARK 6:30–44

Herod, the son of a previous wicked ruler also named Herod, now sat on the throne. He captured and killed one of Jesus' most dedicated helpers, John the Baptist.

When Jesus heard this sad news, he wanted to be alone.

To escape the crowd, Jesus and a few of his friends climbed into a boat. They headed to a deserted place. But when the people saw Jesus leave, they ran ahead.

When Jesus arrived, a multitude of people had already gathered. Jesus felt kindly toward the people, so he began to teach.

Late in the day, Jesus' helpers urged him to send the people away from the remote area to find food. There were about five thousand men, plus women and children, and there was nowhere nearby to find something to eat.

But Jesus answered, "The people don't need to leave. You can give them something to eat."

The disciples said, "We only have five small loaves of bread and two fish. If we are going to feed all these people, we will have to buy food."

Jesus said, "Have the people sit in groups of fifty."

And so the crowd divided up into smaller groups.

Jesus then took the five small loaves and two fish. He looked up to heaven, gave thanks, and broke apart the food into smaller pieces.

The disciples distributed the fish and bread among the people.

Everyone ate as much as they wanted. The leftovers filled twelve baskets.

KEY VERSE

Therefore I tell you, do not worry about your life, what you will eat or drink; or about your body, what you will wear. Is not life more than food, and the body more than clothes? **Matthew 6:25**

TALK ABOUT IT

- When a crowd gathers at a baseball stadium, where do they get food?

- When relatives come to your house, where do they eat?

- When you want to "eat out" or "pick up," where do you go?

PRAY TOGETHER

Dear God, In the morning, I like to eat ___. My favorite lunch is ___. And for supper I like ___. Thank you, God, for healthy food. Amen.

NOTE TO PARENTS

How would you rate your child's manners?

Previous generations of parents taught etiquette when gathered around the family dinner table. Today, our "grab and go" approach to mealtime allows fewer opportunities to teach a child how to set the table and the reason for a napkin.

The table manners your child uses today will go with them as they grow up. What is your child taking from the dinner table?

THE GOOD FRIEND: THE STORY OF THE GOOD SAMARITAN

Luke 10:25–37

People can disappoint us, avoid us, and surprise us. In this story, you will meet one person who disappoints and another who avoids a situation. But this sad story ends happily when a third person comes onto the scene.

FAST FACTS

Travelers, who carried only a walking stick, money bag, and water cup, could be robbed by thieves who hid behind boulders or bushes.

LUKE 10:25–37

One day when Jesus was teaching, a lawyer stood up in the crowd. He asked the question, "What should I do to live forever in heaven?"

Jesus said, "What does the Bible say?" The lawyer answered, "Love God and love your neighbor." Jesus said, "That's right."

Then the man asked another question, "Who is my neighbor?"

Jesus answered the lawyer by telling this story:

"A man was robbed while traveling on the road. The thieves grabbed everything he had, beat him, and left him half dead.

"A priest happened to be walking on the same road. When he saw the injured man, he avoided him by walking on the other side of the road.

"Another man came by. He was a priest's assistant. When he saw the injured man, he also walked on the other side of the road.

"Then a foreigner rode past. When he saw the injured man, he stopped. He climbed off his donkey and bandaged the wounds of the injured man. He lifted the man onto the donkey and took him to a nearby inn. The foreigner paid the innkeeper to care for the man and promised to return and pay for the extra costs."

The story ended here, but Jesus asked the lawyer, "Which of these three people was a good neighbor?"

The lawyer answered, "The man who showed kindness and compassion."

Jesus said, "Go and do the same."

KEY VERSE

Dear children, let us not love with words or speech but with actions and in truth. **1 John 3:18**

TALK ABOUT IT

- Which of the three men in this story would you have expected to help the injured traveler? Why?

- What are the qualities of a good neighbor?

- In what ways are you a good neighbor?

PRAY TOGETHER

Dear God, Sometimes I don't pay attention to people around me. Sometimes I don't try to help when someone needs it. Help me to be aware of people's needs and help when I am able. Amen.

NOTE TO PARENTS

Helping others by being socially responsible is a recurring theme in schools and churches. As a result, children are often asked to contribute a minimum number of hours to community service projects or ministries. Requesting donations of a child's time usually requires time and sometimes money from parents, too. Although some parents resent this "legislation of service," when possible, take this opportunity to meet other parents. For example, you might serve with other parents when the fifth-graders are asked to spend a morning picking up trash along the highway.

When children are younger, we have numerous opportunities to get to know other parents through class parties and activities. But as children grow up and travel to games on buses, those opportunities to meet other parents diminish. Participation in service projects with your child not only models being a good neighbor but also helps build your personal parent network.

TWO SISTERS: THE STORY OF MARTHA AND MARY

Luke 10:38-42

If Jesus came to your house, what would you do? Clean your room (even the closet)? Give the dog a bath so he smelled nice? Wear your nicest clothes? All of that would be good, but the most important part of the visit would be the time you spent listening to Jesus. That's the lesson one of the women learns in this story.

FAST FACTS

Sit down! In Bible times, people would sit on the floor around a piece of leather or skin on which the food was served.

LUKE 10:38–42

Jesus and his disciples were traveling to Jerusalem. About two miles away, they stopped in a village to visit their friends Mary and Martha.

Martha welcomed them into their home. Then she got busy in the kitchen.

Martha poured drinks from a tall pitcher. She set out fresh bread, honey, and figs on the table, and then she realized her sister was missing. Martha wondered why her sister wasn't helping her prepare the food. "Mary?" she called.

Turning around, Martha found her sister sitting at the feet of Jesus. He was telling her about the kingdom of God. Frustrated that her sister appeared lazy and had left her with the work of preparing a big dinner, Martha complained to Jesus.

"Lord, doesn't it bother you that Mary has left me with all the work? Tell her to come and help me."

"Martha, Martha," Jesus said gently. "Don't worry about serving fish with all the trimmings. It isn't important. A simple meal is fine. Mary has chosen to learn about God. That's what matters."

KEY VERSE

Show me your ways, Lord, teach me your paths. **Psalm 25:4**

TALK ABOUT IT

- A title should give the reader an idea about the story or interest you in the story.

- Do you think "Two Sisters" is a good title for this story? What are two other possible titles for this story?

- Household chores distracted Martha from learning. What keeps you from learning about Jesus?

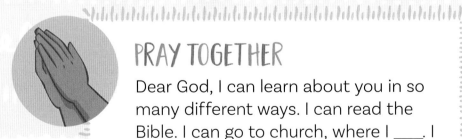

PRAY TOGETHER

Dear God, I can learn about you in so many different ways. I can read the Bible. I can go to church, where I ___. I can watch what people do when they are filled with love for you, like ___. Help me believe so that others see I love you, too. Amen.

NOTE TO PARENTS

As wise parents, we learn from our children and with them, too.

A child frequently teaches us lessons about patience, gentleness, and flexibility that are sometimes hard to learn. A child who is exuberant models joy for us, and a child who is responsible models self-discipline. In our child we see examples of many godly virtues.

But we can also learn *with* a child. Perhaps you're doing that as you read through this book. Maybe you're hearing a Bible story for the first time or from a different perspective. Perhaps one of these parent notes has struck a responsive chord, or a key verse that your child repeats during the day echoes in your head, too.

As wise parents, we learn from our children and with them, too. What will you learn today?

THE MAN WHO SAID THANK YOU: THE STORY OF A GRATEFUL LEPER

Luke 17:11–19

Are you thankful for the sunshine today? Thankful for the rain? Thankful for snow to make snowballs? When we realize how much God gives us, our thankfulness spills over and becomes a smile. In this story, ten men smiled, but only one said "thank you" to God.

FAST FACTS

To keep skin disease from spreading, sick people, including those with leprosy, were required to live with other sick people, away from their families.

LUKE 17:11–19

Jesus and his disciples traveled to many places and met many people. One day, on their way to Jerusalem, they approached a village. Standing off in the distance, they saw a group of ten men.

One of the men was a foreigner.

All ten men had leprosy, a horrible skin disease.

To prevent the disease from spreading, they could not touch healthy people. The lepers were forbidden from even standing near others, so they called out to Jesus, "Master, have pity on us. Help us."

Jesus looked at them and called back, "Go and show yourselves to the priests."

As the sick men walked down the road toward the priests, they talked with one another. Then they looked at one another. The sores were gone. Their skin was healthy.

Jesus had healed them!

The men dropped their crutches. They unwrapped the bandages and waved their arms. They clapped and shouted that Jesus had made them well.

When the foreigner in the group saw
that he had been healed, he left
the others and returned to Jesus.
Shouting praises to God, he fell at
Jesus' feet. The foreigner thanked
Jesus repeatedly for the gift of a
healthy body.

Jesus asked, "Weren't ten men
healed? Where are the other nine?
Why did only one come back to
thank God?"

Then Jesus told the man, "You may
get up and go. Your faith has made
you well."

KEY VERSE

Give thanks in all circumstances; for this is God's will for you in Christ Jesus.
1 Thessalonians 5:18

TALK ABOUT IT

- Some people think this is a good story to read on Thanksgiving.

- Do you agree? Why or why not?

- What do you like best about Thanksgiving Day?

- Some people suggest that those who love God should practice "thanksgiving." What do you think that means?

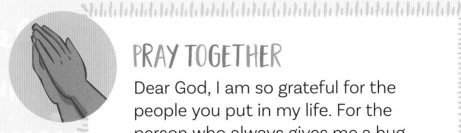

PRAY TOGETHER

Dear God, I am so grateful for the people you put in my life. For the person who always gives me a hug, ___, and for someone who makes me smile, ___. I am especially thankful for you, because you ___. Amen.

NOTE TO PARENTS

Thanksgiving is a minor holiday for children. Although children enjoy most celebrations, the reality is that Thanksgiving has become breathing space before December.

Thanksgiving traditions can help children focus attention on God's gifts. That's the reason some families place a muffin cup with five kernels of corn at each place on the holiday dinner table. The kernels are a reminder of the harsh times the Pilgrims endured before the first Thanksgiving but can also trigger thoughts of five current blessings from God. Other families fill an empty cornucopia centerpiece with index cards on which dinner guests have written the blessings for which they are thankful. Traditions may be the glue that holds families together, but at Thanksgiving, they can also remind us of God's gifts, including the gift of each other.

JESUS WELCOMES THE CHILDREN:
THE STORY OF CHILDREN BEING BLESSED BY JESUS

Matthew 19:13–15

It's fun to receive an invitation. But how do you feel if someone says, "You can't come"? That's what happens in this story. People tell children, "You can't come to see Jesus." What do you think Jesus says?

FAST FACTS

In Bible times, boys and girls did not go to school together.

Boys were taught by rabbis in a classroom attached to the synagogue.

Girls learned from their mothers how to cook and care for a house.

MATTHEW 19:13–15

Jesus and his helpers continued to travel throughout the countryside. Whether Jesus spoke inside a house or stopped by a well, in a big city or a small village, in the morning or later in the day, people came.

Wherever Jesus went, people followed.

And they kept coming.

One day, mothers carried their infants through the crowd to reach the place where Jesus was teaching. They wanted him to bless their children. The adults smiled as toddlers wobbled unsteadily toward Jesus. Older children held the hands of younger children as they wove their way through the crowd.

Parents were eager for all the children to receive a blessing. But some of

Jesus' helpers were displeased.

"Jesus should be healing the sick," grumbled one man.

"Jesus should spend his time teaching adults," muttered another.

The helpers didn't want Jesus to be bothered, so they stepped forward to shoo away the children.

But when Jesus saw what was happening, he stretched out his arms toward the children.

He turned to his helpers and said, "Let the children come to me. Don't try to stop them."

Hearing these words, little ones raced into his open arms.

Gently, Jesus leaned down to welcome even the smallest.

As tenderly as any father cradles his children, Jesus wrapped his arms around them.

Jesus explained, "People who are like these children belong in God's kingdom."

Then Jesus reached out to touch the head of each child in blessing.

KEY VERSE

Jesus said, "Let the little children come to me, and do not hinder them, for the kingdom of heaven belongs to such as these." **Matthew 9:14**

TALK ABOUT IT

- If you had been among the children who received a blessing from Jesus that day long ago, would that have changed your life?

- If so, how?

- In what way does God bless you today?

PRAY TOGETHER

Dear God, When I talk to you like this, I feel ____. Even if I am upset, discouraged, frustrated, or tired, I know you will listen to what I say. That makes me feel ____. Amen.

NOTE TO PARENTS

As you read the stories in this book, does your child ask questions you can't answer?

When children are young, we can answer most of their questions, or at least respond with enough words to satisfy their curiosity. But as children grow up, they realize we don't know everything.

It can be humbling to admit, "I don't know," but that transparency gives us an "excuse" to learn together with our child. That's something we might need, because as a child grows up, those casual, relaxed conversations that overflowed during the early years become less frequent and shorter. Discussions triggered by stories in this book offer an opportunity to exchange thoughts, ideas, and concepts that shape a child's value system. Our participation in these conversations also demonstrates that growing in our faith, studying the Bible, and learning about God are parts of a lifelong process.

THE GENEROUS TAX COLLECTOR:
THE STORY OF ZACCHAEUS

Luke 19:1–10

A generous person gives because
they want to share. They don't need
a present or a prize in return. This is a
story about a man who learned to be
generous. Would you be described as
a generous person?

FAST FACTS

The sycamore is a fig tree that
bears fruit several times each year.

Sycamore tree branches grow
wide and close to the ground, so
Zacchaeus had an easy climb.

LUKE 19:1–10

Jesus continued to heal and teach as he traveled throughout the region. Of course, crowds followed Jesus everywhere he went.

One day he came to the city of Jericho. Here, the crowd overflowed the road and spilled into the countryside.

A rich man from town named Zacchaeus found himself at the back of the crowd. Zacchaeus was a tax collector in the town. Tax collectors like Zacchaeus were unpopular because they sometimes cheated people.

But Zacchaeus had heard about Jesus and was curious to see him. People in the crowd towered above Zacchaeus, because he was a short man.

When he could not see Jesus above the crowd, Zacchaeus ran ahead and

scrambled up into a sycamore tree.
His high position would give him a
clear view of Jesus.

From his perch, Zacchaeus could
clearly see the people swarming
around Jesus as he walked down
the road. When he reached the
tree, Jesus looked up and said,
"Zacchaeus, hurry down. I want to
come to your house."

Zacchaeus slid down the trunk, then
scurried home quickly. He wanted to
prepare a proper welcome for Jesus.

People in the crowd complained, "Jesus is going to eat with a man who sins."

Later that day, Zacchaeus told Jesus, "Lord, I am giving half of everything I own to the poor. If I have cheated someone, I will pay back four times more than I owe."

And Jesus was pleased with his generous spirit.

KEY VERSE

Each of you should give what you have decided in your heart to give, not reluctantly or under compulsion, for God loves a cheerful giver. **2 Corinthians 9:7**

TALK ABOUT IT

- Why might someone say, "Zacchaeus was short, but he stood tall in the eyes of the Lord"?

- Do you think it was hard for Zacchaeus to be so generous? Why or why not?

- Is it harder or easier for a rich person to be generous?

- When can you remember being generous?

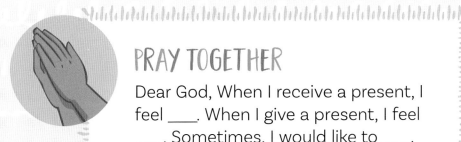

PRAY TOGETHER

Dear God, When I receive a present, I feel ___. When I give a present, I feel ___. Sometimes, I would like to ___. Help me to feel good about sharing what you give me. Amen.

NOTE TO PARENTS

When children are young, we teach them the basics of fiscal literacy: save, spend, give, and invest. But stewardship is more than filling an offering envelope. Stewardship, or managing what the Lord has given to us, includes sharing treasures, time, and talent.

Older children can develop empathy, or the ability to identify with the feelings of another person, when they practice good stewardship. Volunteering in the church nursery or helping pass offering baskets during a worship service is not just good for a congregation; it's also good for the child. When the joy of giving is discovered during childhood, it is often embraced as a lifelong value.

A PARADE FOR JESUS:
THE STORY OF PALM SUNDAY

Matthew 21:1–11

This story is about a parade. There were no marching bands, floats, or balloons, but there were tree branches. What kind of parade was that? Read this story to find out.

FAST FACTS

The day that Jesus rode into Jerusalem is commonly called Palm Sunday, which refers to the branches people spread on the road (John 12:13).

MATTHEW 21:1–11

Long before Jesus was born in Bethlehem, an old prophet said that God's chosen king would arrive riding a donkey.

The prophet said this was going to happen even though most kings galloped on powerful horses.

This story tells how the words of the prophet came true.

Jesus and his disciples were traveling to Jerusalem at a busy time of year. Many people were coming for a weeklong festival.

Jesus sent two of his helpers to a village to find a donkey and its colt.

The men found them just as Jesus had described. They put blankets on the animals and led them to Jesus.

Even though no one had ever ridden the donkey, it stood steady as Jesus climbed on.

Travelers who were coming to Jerusalem for the holiday had heard that Jesus might also arrive.

"Jesus is coming. Jesus is coming," people said with excitement.

Even before Jesus entered the city, people walked through the narrow streets waving branches they had stripped from palm trees. Then Jesus came riding through the city on the donkey.

When he appeared, the crowds grew denser. There were so many people, some could not even see Jesus, so they simply waved branches high above their heads.

"Hosanna, hosanna," the people said.

Some laid their coats down in the street, so the donkey walked on a carpet of cloth. Others laid down their palm branches.

Everywhere people greeted Jesus, saying, "Hosanna! Blessed is he who comes in the name of the Lord. Hosanna in the highest!"

Everything happened just as the old prophet had written.

The crowds that went ahead of him and those that followed shouted, "Hosanna to the Son of David!" "Blessed is he who comes in the name of the Lord!" "Hosanna in the highest heaven!" **Matthew 21:9**

TALK ABOUT IT

• In the story, who said this?

"Hosanna!"
"Bring me a colt."
"The Savior of the world will arrive riding a donkey."
"Jesus is coming!"

• Now put these quotes in order.

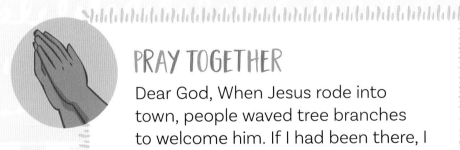

PRAY TOGETHER

Dear God, When Jesus rode into town, people waved tree branches to welcome him. If I had been there, I might have ____. Help me to welcome you into my heart. Amen.

NOTE TO PARENTS

Everyone loves a parade, except an older child who feels they've outgrown such childish delights. With the strong influence of pop culture on clothing, music, media, entertainment, and activities, many parents feel children grow up too quickly.

How can you respond to a child who feels too grown-up to enjoy age-appropriate activities? Pair the older child with a younger child. This allows the older child to enjoy the activity while in a peer-acceptable position. Or ask your child to invite classmates to participate, too. Because some older children are just developing the confidence needed to go solo in social situations, they find safety and security when surrounded by peers.

Give your child opportunities to have fun in the privacy of your home, doing things that your child honestly likes but wouldn't publicly admit to enjoying. This reminds an older child that there are many ways to have fun.

ARRESTED! THE STORY OF JUDAS'S BETRAYAL

Matthew 26:17–56

Jesus was the kindest person to ever live, and yet this story begins a very sad chapter in his life. What happened to Jesus wasn't fair, but it was part of God's good plan.

FAST FACTS

Gethsemane, where Jesus went to pray, was a garden at the base of a mountain, the Mount of Olives, where olive trees grow.

MATTHEW 26:17–56

After the parade through Jerusalem, Jesus told his disciples that he would soon die. Jesus knew that religious leaders and the chief priests were meeting in secret, plotting to kill him. At this time, the disciples did not understand that Jesus' death was a part of God's plan.

On Thursday evening, the twelve disciples gathered with Jesus in the upper room of a house. While they ate, Jesus spoke again about his death, saying, "One of you who is eating here will hand me over to my enemies."

During the meal, Jesus blessed the food. He knew this was the last supper they would share. They sang a hymn and then, as usual, went to

pray at the Mount of Olives.

When they came to the garden called Gethsemane, Jesus told the disciples, "Sit here while I pray."

Three of them walked farther into the garden with him. As they walked, Jesus grew even more sorrowful, because he knew what would soon happen. He told Peter, James, and John to stay and watch as he prayed.

Then Jesus walked a little farther, fell to the ground, and prayed mightily to his heavenly Father.

Jesus retuned and found the three disciples sleeping. After waking Peter, Jesus again went away to pray. The same thing happened a second time.

When he returned a third time, Jesus woke the disciples and said, "Let's go. The one who will turn me over to my enemies is here."

And with those words, Judas, one of the twelve, approached through the darkness with a mob of men clutching clubs and swords. Judas walked right up to Jesus and kissed him. The kiss signaled to the officials that Jesus was the person to grab.

Jesus was arrested, and his disciples ran away through the darkness.

KEY VERSE

But I trust in you, Lord; I say, "You are my God." My times are in your hands; deliver me from the hands of my enemies, from those who pursue me.
Psalm 31:14–15

TALK ABOUT IT

The scenes in this story take place in various locations:

- What was the city?

- Where did Jesus and his disciplines share the last supper?

- To what mountain did Jesus and his disciples go to pray?

- In what garden was Jesus arrested?

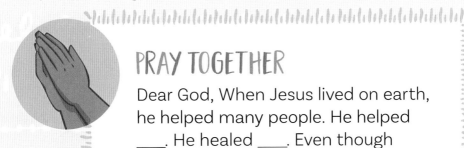

PRAY TOGETHER

Dear God, When Jesus lived on earth, he helped many people. He helped ___. He healed ___. Even though Jesus is with you in heaven, I know he is still helping people like me. Thank you for Jesus. Amen.

NOTE TO PARENTS

"It's not fair." That three-word sentence echoes through daily life with an older child. The unfairness that Jesus, the perfect Son of God, was arrested for doing nothing wrong is a discussion point that might emerge with your child from this story. Because preadolescents may often think that the world has ganged up against them, this might be a point of identification with Jesus.

A feeling of sadness is the other common reaction to this story for older children. Even though we know the events of Good Friday were part of God's plan of salvation, the arrest of Jesus begins a portion of the Bible that triggers deep sadness. Encourage your children to talk about their feelings after this story, then read the following two stories to complete the happenings of Holy Week.

DARK FRIDAY:
THE STORY OF JESUS' DEATH

Matthew 26:57–27:56

The people who lived in Jerusalem had a choice: they could vote against Jesus or vote against a murderer. Although the people made a bad choice, Jesus forgave them.

FAST FACTS

Beginning at noon on the day Jesus died, the sky was dark for three hours (Matthew 27:51).

Jesus was crucified on a hill called Golgotha, which means *skull* (John 19:17).

MATTHEW 26:57–27:56

After Jesus was arrested, he was led to the palace of the high priest. The chief priests were jealous of Jesus and wanted him killed, so they brought people to court who lied about him. The priests badgered Jesus with questions, but he was silent.

Finally, the chief priest asked, "Are you the Christ, Son of the Living God?"

Jesus answered, "I am."

Then some of the leaders started to spit on Jesus. They blindfolded him and hit him.

Early the next morning, the priests and leaders decided that Jesus should die. They tied him up and led him to the governor.

A huge crowd had gathered outside the governor's palace. The priests and leaders started to stir up the people, suggesting that Jesus should be killed. The mob started to shout and yell.

The governor followed a tradition of letting the people choose to free one prisoner from jail. When he asked if the mob wanted to free Jesus or Barabbas, a terrorist, the people shouted, "Barabbas, Barabbas!"

Then the governor asked, "What should I do with him who is called King of the Jews?"

Even though Jesus had done nothing wrong, the crowd still shouted, "Crucify him, crucify him!"

So the governor, wanting to please the people, said, "Take this man away."

The soldiers led Jesus to a hill outside the city. They hammered a big cross into a hill, hung Jesus on the cross, and left him to die.

KEY VERSE

But God demonstrates his own love for us in this: While we were still sinners, Christ died for us. **Romans 5:8**

TALK ABOUT IT

- After someone dies, people say they are grieving or mourning.

- What do those words mean?

- Sometimes there is a funeral after a person dies. What happens at a funeral?

- Have you ever known someone who died?

PRAY TOGETHER

Dear God, When I hear about what happened to Jesus, I feel ___. I want to know ___. Thank you for listening to my prayer. Amen.

NOTE TO PARENTS

Even if older children have not had a close personal experience with death, they have probably learned some basic facts. They know death is not contagious, that it is a fact of life, and that people often cry in response to a death.

When talking about loss or any sensitive subject, follow your child's lead. If your child does not want to talk or even respond to the discussion questions accompanying this story, that's fine, too. They know you are available and open to a future discussion.

Many parents wait until an event triggers a necessary conversation, but discussing end-of-life issues should not be delayed. We listen more attentively and answer more thoughtfully when we are not stressed or emotionally involved in a situation.

GOOD NEWS: THE STORY OF JESUS' RESURRECTION

Matthew 28:1–10

When Jesus' helpers woke up on the first Easter morning, they were still sad. But their tears of sadness became tears of joy after the women went to the tomb. Why was this Sunday such a happy day? Read the very best news story ever.

FAST FACTS

Mary Magdalene is mentioned fourteen times in the Bible.

The biblical list of names for Jesus goes almost from A to Z: from "the last Adam" (1 Corinthians 15:45) to "the Word" (John 1:1).

MATTHEW 28:1–10

After Jesus died, his body was placed in a tomb. A huge stone was rolled in front of the entrance. Armed guards stood outside.

On the third day after Jesus' death, Mary Magdalene and another Mary arrived at the tomb just before dawn. Suddenly, a strong earthquake rocked the ground. An angel of the Lord came down from heaven, rolled the huge stone away from the tomb, and sat on the big rock.

The soldiers who stood guard shook, then collapsed to the earth.

The angel told Jesus' friends, "Don't be afraid. I know you are looking for Jesus. He is not here. He is risen, as he said."

The women listened as the angel said, "Now hurry! Tell his disciples that he has been raised to life. Jesus is on his way to Galilee. Go there, and you will see him."

The women hurried from the tomb, still fearful but also joyful. Then suddenly, Jesus met them. The women held on to him and worshipped him.

Jesus repeated what the angel had said. Gently he told them, "Don't be afraid. Go and tell the disciples to meet me in Galilee."

And the women ran to share the good news.

KEY VERSE

For God so loved the world that he gave his one and only Son, that whoever believes in him shall not perish but have eternal life. **John 3:16**

TALK ABOUT IT

- If you had written a newspaper headline for the first Easter, what would it have said?

- Why do you think some news reports today feature so much bad news?

- When you have good news, who do you tell?

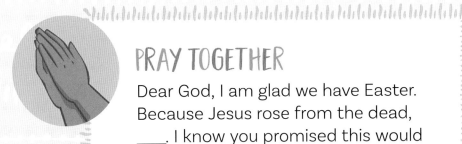

PRAY TOGETHER

Dear God, I am glad we have Easter. Because Jesus rose from the dead, ___. I know you promised this would happen, and I'm so glad it did. After hearing the story of the first Easter, I ___. Hallelujah! Amen.

NOTE TO PARENTS

Reading the story of Easter during any season of the year places emphasis on the resurrection of Jesus. This is an ideal time to ask yourself, "What does my child know?" You and your child might even list all of the facts you know about our Lord and Savior.

If your child's list is missing important concepts, plan to fill in the gaps. But don't just do this with facts. Biblical literacy for older children goes beyond knowing about Bible heroes. Help your children take the next step and apply biblical truths to real life, as they do throughout this book. When talking about faith-related issues, be open to your child's questions or even ask some of your own. You might be surprised by your child's insights.

During these years, academic learning is prioritized at school. Learning about Jesus can be prioritized at home.

JESUS RETURNS TO HEAVEN: THE STORY OF JESUS' ASCENSION

Luke 24:13–53; Acts 1:3–11

When you look up, does bright sunshine make you squint? Do you see a cloud drift across the blue sky? When Jesus' helpers looked up, they saw an amazing sight.

FAST FACTS

Thomas, one of Jesus' helpers, was probably a twin (John 11:16).

The New Testament was originally written in Greek on papyrus. The word *paper* comes from *papyrus.*

LUKE 24:13–53; ACTS 1:3–11

After Jesus rose from the dead, many people saw him. After appearing to Mary and other women in the garden on Easter morning, he met two of his disciples on the road to a village.

Then he talked with the eleven disciples when they were eating.

Jesus even went fishing and ate breakfast with some of his friends on a beach.

Altogether, Jesus spent forty days with his disciples, talking about the kingdom of heaven.

One day, Jesus was teaching his eleven disciples near the top of a mountain. Jesus raised his hands and blessed them.

As he was speaking, a cloud floated down and hid Jesus. The disciples stared intently into the sky.

Suddenly, two angels dressed in white stood in front of them.

The angels said, "Why do you stand here looking into the sky? This same Jesus, who has been taken from you into heaven, will return."

The disciples fell down on their knees to worship their risen and ascended Savior.

They returned to the temple in Jerusalem, where they praised God.

Then they went out, preaching the good news of Jesus everywhere.

KEY VERSE

"Men of Galilee," they said, "why do you stand here looking into the sky? This same Jesus, who has been taken from you into heaven, will come back in the same way you have seen him go into heaven." **Acts 1:11**

TALK ABOUT IT

- Jesus taught his disciples by talking with them.

- Do you learn best when you hear, read, or write new information?

- Originally, Jesus had twelve disciples. Why were only eleven disciples with him on the mountain?

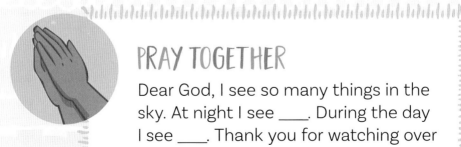

PRAY TOGETHER

Dear God, I see so many things in the sky. At night I see ___. During the day I see ___. Thank you for watching over me from heaven. Amen.

NOTE TO PARENTS

"What is heaven like?"

A child may ask that question after hearing the story of Jesus' ascension. Although we aren't sure specifically what heaven looks like or even exactly where heaven is, we know that *paradise* is another word for heaven. When discussing heaven, ask your child to imagine the most wonderful place in the world, then remind her that heaven will be even better! When a child asks, "Will I have a dog in heaven?" or "Will I be the best baseball player in heaven?" assure her that God will provide whatever she needs. Those words can comfort a child and comfort us.

GOD'S SPIRIT COMES:
THE STORY OF PENTECOST

Acts 2:1-47

The Bible tells us that a man named Peter was a great preacher. Sometimes, he preached to large crowds of people. One day, Peter preached to thousands, but the big crowd wasn't the big story that day.

FAST FACTS

Pentecost was more than wind and flames: people spoke in fifteen different languages (Acts 2:9-11).

Pentecost was fifty days after Easter.

ACTS 2:1–47

After Jesus' return to heaven, the disciples and other followers continued to talk about him. They prayed together and waited for the gift of the Holy Spirit, which Jesus had promised they would receive.

The streets of Jerusalem were crowded with people gathering to celebrate a thanksgiving harvest festival. Pilgrims had traveled from all over, so conversations took place in many different languages.

Early on a Sunday morning, Jesus' disciples and many of his friends and followers were praying together in a large room.

Suddenly, there was a noise from heaven like a rush of a mighty wind. Then tongues that looked like fire appeared above each person's head.

Just as Jesus had promised, his followers were now filled with the Holy Spirit.

Outside the house, the crowds had heard the noise and wondered what was happening inside the building.

Jesus' followers began speaking in many languages, so everyone understood as they listened to the wonderful things God had done. Some people thought the disciples were drunk.

But Peter said, "We can speak in your languages because God has given us the Holy Spirit. Weeks ago, you crucified Jesus, the Son of God. But he did not stay dead. He is alive."

The crowd was silent. Then some people began feeling sorry for what they had done to Jesus. They cried out, "What can we do?"

Peter answered, "Turn back to God. Be baptized, so your sins will be forgiven."

About three thousand people believed Peter's message and were baptized.

KEY VERSE

Because you are his [children], God sent the Spirit of his Son into our hearts, the Spirit who calls out, "*Abba*, Father." **Galations 4:6**

TALK ABOUT IT

- What languages do you speak every day?

- How do you feel when someone speaks a language you don't understand?

- What could you do to learn another language?

- Which language would you like to learn?

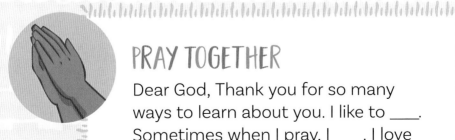

PRAY TOGETHER

Dear God, Thank you for so many ways to learn about you. I like to ___. Sometimes when I pray, I ___. I love you, God. Amen.

NOTE TO PARENTS

The same Spirit that filled the disciples at the first Pentecost is within every child of God. That's because moms, dads, grandparents, and all who believe in Jesus are children of God. The key verse accompanying the story highlights this fact.

When our children were young, we often reached to hold their hand. That's what a good parent does. As our Father, God does that for us, regardless of how old we are. The Holy Spirit will guide our actions when we are sleep-deprived, our thoughts when we face jealousy, and our words when we cope with a child's disobedience. There is no time warp between the first Pentecost and today.

As the psalmist reminds us, "The Lord will hold your hand, and if you stumble, you still won't fall" (Psalm 37:24).

WAITING AT THE GATE:
THE STORY OF PETER AND JOHN

Acts 3:1–10

In this story, a man is asking people for donations because he can't walk, so he cannot work. God gives the man something better than money. Read to see what God gave him.

FAST FACTS

Peter and John were ministry partners. They prepared the Passover for Jesus (Luke 22:8) and watched his trial (John 18:15). On Easter Day, they ran together to the tomb (John 20:1–9).

ACTS 3:1–10

At three o'clock one day, Peter and John, Jesus' helpers, went to the temple to pray. As the men neared the Beautiful Gate, they marveled at its massive structure, gleaming in the afternoon sun.

A man who couldn't walk sat in front, because he was not allowed inside.

Every day, his friends brought him to sit by the Beautiful Gate. Before worshippers entered, the man would ask for money.

That's what happened when Peter and John neared the gate. They stopped in front of him. Hopeful they would help him, the man waited.

But instead of dipping into his pocket for a coin, Peter said, "Look at us." The man looked up.

Peter said, "I don't have silver or gold, but I will give you what I have. In the name of Jesus Christ, get up and walk."

Then Peter reached forward to help the man stand.

Immediately, the man's feet and ankles became strong. He stood. Then he started walking.

He walked with Peter and John into the temple, leaping and shouting and praising God.

Everyone who saw the man knew that he couldn't walk. People were amazed. They had no idea what had happened to make him walk. A crowd gathered.

Peter asked the people, "Why are you surprised? This man put his faith in the name of Jesus. Faith in Jesus made him well."

KEY VERSE

But you are a chosen people, a royal priesthood, a holy nation, God's special possession, that you may declare the praises of him who called you out of darkness into his wonderful light. **1 Peter 2:9**

TALK ABOUT IT

- The beggar could not walk, so his friends carried him to the temple.

- Do you know someone who uses a wheelchair or who has trouble walking?

- How is their life more difficult than yours?

- What is one way you could be kind to a person who has a physical disability?

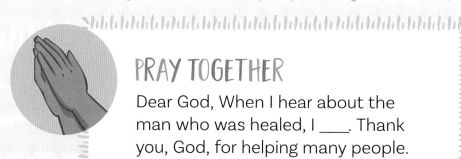

PRAY TOGETHER

Dear God, When I hear about the man who was healed, I ____. Thank you, God, for helping many people. Amen.

NOTE TO PARENTS

How do you respond to someone who is homeless or someone with an obvious need? Your child will not only observe what you say and do but will probably adopt the same behavior.

Some parents feel guilty or are personally uncomfortable when they see a person who is less fortunate. Other parents try to avoid such situations or make a quick donation. But increasingly, parents are choosing to involve children in acts of compassion.

Empathy, or the ability to make an emotional connection and understand what a person feels, develops gradually as a child grows up. When a parent uses teachable moments, a child can develop sensitivity toward others and learn to respond in developmentally and socially appropriate ways.

THE JAILBREAK:
THE STORY OF PAUL AND SILAS

Acts 16:25–34

Paul and Silas traveled from city to city talking about Jesus, although people were not always happy to hear their message. When they went to the city of Philippi, they ended up in jail. But as you'll see, they weren't even imprisoned for a whole night.

FAST FACTS

Paul was a tentmaker (Acts 18:3).

The thirteen letters that Paul wrote to churches and church leaders form a large part of the New Testament.

ACTS 16:25–34

Paul carefully leaned back against the prison wall. Creatures of all kinds moved behind him. Wondering if the scurrying sound was a rat looking for supper, Paul tried to get more comfortable. The heavy chains on his ankles made it hard to move.

The jail cell was dark, smelly, and damp, but he and Silas were still thankful to God.

Around midnight, the two men started singing songs of praise.

The other prisoners listened. They were amazed and wondered, "Why would prisoners praise God?"

Suddenly, the earth shook. The earthquake was so violent, the prison doors flung open. The prisoners' chains were loosened.

When the jailer saw that the prison had collapsed, he panicked. Worried that his prisoners had escaped, the jailer yelled for someone to bring a light.

Cautiously he headed into the crumbling building. Paul called out through the darkness and said, "We're still here."

The jailer stepped over broken walls and climbed down shattered stairs until he reached the cell where Paul and Silas calmly sat.

Kneeling in front of the men, the jailer asked, "What must I do to be saved?" Paul said, "Believe in Jesus." Then the jailer listened as Paul talked about Jesus.

The jailer led the men out of the prison and took them home with him. There he helped Paul and Silas get comfortable and served them food.

Everyone in the household listened to Paul and Silas speak about Jesus, and the jailer's whole family believed what they said.

KEY VERSE

They replied, "Believe in the Lord Jesus, and you will be saved—you and your household." **Acts 6:31**

TALK ABOUT IT

- Paul and Silas were tossed into prison because they told people about Jesus.

- Was that fair to them?

- Is life always fair?

- When have you been in a situation and said, "It's not fair"?

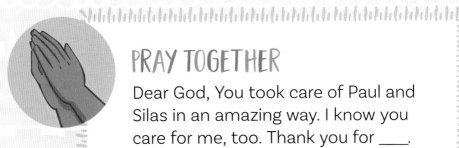

PRAY TOGETHER

Dear God, You took care of Paul and Silas in an amazing way. I know you care for me, too. Thank you for ____. Amen.

NOTE TO PARENTS

We can't force a child to believe in Jesus as Savior and Lord, but we can pray that God would open our child's heart to receive God's message.

We can also share God's word, model godly living, and integrate Christian lifestyle elements, like you are doing through this book, into daily activities. These are ways we follow the biblical direction for parents that Paul records in his letter to the people of Ephesus (Ephesians 6:4).

A WONDERFUL SIGHT:
THE STORY OF JOHN'S REVELATION

Revelation 1, 21, 22

After Jesus went to heaven, one of his friends had a marvelous dream. He saw Jesus. The man even caught a glimpse of heaven. What do you think heaven looks like?

FAST FACTS

People in seven different churches read the book of Revelation. The churches were connected by a major road (Revelation 1:11).

REVELATION 1, 21, 22

Jesus' disciples continued to preach God's good news. Most of the people they taught had not personally met Jesus, but the disciples described miraculous things he had done. They talked about the people he had healed, and they preached about Jesus' victory over sin and death that he earned for us on the cross.

Many of the rulers at the time did not like people to hear about Jesus. One wicked king wanted people to worship him instead of the one true God.

During this time, many people became Christians even though it was dangerous. Wicked rulers often captured those who believed in the true God. Some Christians were even killed. Jesus' helpers were captured and thrown in prison.

This is what happened to John: a disciple Jesus loved very much.

John was an old man when he was sent away to the island of Patmos.

One Sunday morning, John heard a loud voice that sounded like a trumpet. He turned toward the voice and saw Jesus. What a magnificent sight! The Lord blazed with glory in a golden robe. He shone as bright as the sun.

John fell to his feet, but Jesus reached out his right hand and said, "Don't be afraid. Listen to what I say. I know all about your hard work. I know you have gone through hard times for me and haven't given up."

Jesus showed John visions, like dreams, of the future. John saw God's holy city. He even caught a glimpse of God himself, sitting on a throne bathed with rainbow lights.

Then Jesus gave John messages for the churches in seven cities.

John wrote down Jesus' words on a scroll.

When John had written down everything, Jesus promised, "I am coming soon."

And John ended his scroll with the words, "Yes, yes. Come, Lord Jesus."

KEY VERSE

"The time has come," he said. "The kingdom of God has come near. Repent and believe the good news!" **Mark 1:15**

TALK ABOUT IT

- This is the last story in the book.

- How do you feel now that you've reached the end?

- What was the best thing about reading this book?

- Was there a story you didn't like? If so, why?

- Which story would you like to read again?

PRAY TOGETHER

Dear God, I think heaven is ___. I know the angels praise you in heaven. The best thing about heaven is ___. Amen.

NOTE TO PARENTS

What's next? Like John, who wrote centuries ago, you've reached an end point.

"The end" can be an interesting milestone. You can look back and see where you've been and what you've learned. When thinking about the stories you've shared from this book, you might consider what went well. If you set a regular time to read with your child, was the time of day appropriate? Did you set aside enough time to discuss the story? What type of talking points triggered the most meaningful conversation?

Endings are also exciting, because something else lies ahead. What tool will you and your child use to support your child's faith?

John ends Revelation with the words "The grace of the Lord Jesus be with God's people" (Revelation 22:21). That prayer offers an appropriate way to conclude these parent notes to you, too.